Human Goodness

Human Goodness

Yi-Fu Tuan

THE UNIVERSITY OF WISCONSIN PRESS

The University of Wisconsin Press
1930 Monroe Street, 3rd Floor
Madison, Wisconsin 53711-2059

www.wisc.edu/wisconsinpress/

3 Henrietta Street
London WC2E 8LU, England

1   3   5   4   2

Printed in the United States of America

Library of Congress Cataloging-in-Publication Data
Tuan, Yi-fu, 1930–.
Human goodness / Yi-fu Tuan.
      p.   cm.
Includes bibliographical references and index.
ISBN 0-299-22670-0 (cloth: alk. paper)
1. Virtue.   2. Conduct of life.   I. Title.
      BJ1531.T83   2008
  170´.44—dc22   2007040158

Contents

Preface

It is said that in a story the flawed characters—even the villains—have a certain appeal, whereas the good ones, despite efforts on the part of the author, are boring or inconsequential.[1] Newspaper publishers and editors must think the same, for, inevitably, crimes appear on the front page, whereas good deeds appear, if at all, tucked away in a back section devoted to social gossip. Since publishers want their papers to sell and since they have a pretty good idea of what their readers want, presumably readers in general also favor stories of gore to stories of kindness and valor.

Either a pessimistic or an optimistic interpretation can be given to this attitude. The pessimistic interpretation sees people as cynically wanting their own sour experiences in life, their own bad deeds, confirmed in the world "out there." So I have a lousy job, so I occasionally abuse my spouse, slander my office mate, and cheat on my income tax, but worse things—far worse things—are done by other people. The optimistic interpretation takes the overall decency of life for granted. As the weeks and months go by my mail is delivered, the plumber comes when called, children squirt water playfully at one another, and the neighbors volunteer to feed my cat when I'm away. Good, in other words, is the norm, and we are distressed, shocked, by departures from it.

How do I see my fellow human beings? It occurs to me that I have never addressed this question head-on, even though I have been a student of society and culture for half a century. Nor have I confronted the question of whether I find the gore on the front page more worthy of attention than the small acts of heroism in ordinary lives that are sometimes also reported. Accounts of extreme evil do hold me in thrall: I am morbidly drawn, like many others, to the horrors of the Holocaust. But ordinary human flaws, those that derive from our ingrained egoism, our pathetic need for wealth and fame and for power to lord over others, are, for me, simply boring. This is one reason why I cannot be a sociologist. I have no wish to spend a lifetime trying to describe, numerate, and analyze these all too familiar weaknesses and vanities. When I read fiction and find that it deals with the peccadilloes of society, I stop turning the page. The same happens in real life. I have no patience for gossip, my objection being more aesthetic than moral. All the talk about who is up and who is down is as banal and undignified as nose picking. But good people and good action, whether encountered in life or reaching me indirectly through reports, make me sit up. This, I suppose, means that I am basically a pessimist, someone who takes human veniality and nastiness for granted and so is easily surprised not only by heroic virtue but by just good behavior, even politeness.

"Good" rather than "bad" in human beings is, to me, exciting, and exciting, in part, because of its range of manifestation. That idea, again, is contrary to the common wisdom that "good" is monotonously alike, whereas "bad" or evil is endlessly colorful and various. How many people share *my* view rather than, say, Tolstoy's, who famously asseverated in the opening paragraph of *Anna Karenina,* "All happy [read "good"] families are like one another; each unhappy family is unhappy in its own way"?

I would like to know. One way to find out is to offer vignettes of goodness that I happen to have come across and that have lifted my spirit—if only for a moment—and see whether they have a similar effect on you. These vignettes are grouped under some six-teen headings, each of which addresses or exhibits one type of goodness. The variety of ways of being good or doing good is thus shown. In the nature of the case, most of these vignettes highlight a particular act or state of being, and we cannot know whether it stands alone in the life of an individual or whether there are other acts or states of being like it.

"Vignettes" is followed by "Doing Good in the Midst of Evil." This section differs from "Vignettes" in three ways. First, its loca-tion is southern France, where the people are culturally homoge-neous, in contrast to the individuals cited in "Vignettes," who come from different cultures and times. Second, it is set in an exceptionally dark period in European history, one during which much of the Continent came under Nazi domination, and *not* the more or less normal times under which particular states of goodness or acts of goodness occur. Third, in "Doing Good in the Midst of Evil" the "good" is sustained over a period of years and is not just a one-time action.

Still to be supplied are life stories. It is important to have them, for, in striking contrast to scholars and artists, whom we may judge "good" for just one outstanding work, we do not consider a person "good" for just one kind or heroic act. To be judged "good," a person's whole life must show fairly consistent virtue, for we know only too well that even a rogue can give a turnip to a beggar (Dostoevsky's example) and that even a brutal SS guard can be kind to an inmate when he happens to be in the mood. In my third section, then, I offer brief sketches of six good human beings: Confucius and Socrates (ancient), Mozart and Keats (early modern), and Schweitzer and Weil (modern). They are drawn from very different times and cultures; their ways of being good reinforce the idea that goodness is diversely manifest. On the other hand, despite the differences in time and culture, these individuals, each with a strongly developed personality, have much in common.

Lastly, under "Reflections" I try to see what general conclusions I can draw using the evidence I have presented. A basic issue is the amount of good and evil in the world. Earlier I called myself a pessimist, yet I am drawn to examples of human goodness, an activity that in itself would seem to argue for at least a degree of optimism in me. Stephen Jay Gould, the biologist, is surely being upbeat when he speaks of the "ten thousand acts of kindness" that illuminate the human stage every day, making it—on the whole—a good place for most people.[2] To keep a sort of balance and our sanity, we need to be reminded of this bright view. On the other hand, the evils human beings have done and do are so horrible and unrelenting on nearly every page of world history that we may wonder whether these "ten thousand acts of kindness" are merely *points* of light in a night sky of pitch darkness. The Gospel says, "The light shines in darkness, and the darkness overcomes it not" (John 1:3). Is this all we can hope for, or can we see light actually spreading and overcoming the dark?

In 1986 I published a book called *The Good Life*. Its emphasis is on good places, good ways of making a living, and good societies. What you have now is the sequel. Highlighted this time are not groups but individuals and individual acts. I have always wanted to write on human goodness but refrained from a feeling of inadequacy. In my seventy-fifth year I have at last learned to confront the question, If not now, when? and to see that to wait longer in the hope of greater knowledge is pointless, for no individual, however learned, can possibly give a rounded, comprehensive account of human goodness. And yet I would argue that every human being ought to address it sometime in his or her life. Why? Look at it from a simple, pragmatic point of view. Just think how the quality of our life will improve if we gossip, but gossip in the root meaning of that word, which is to relate "good tidings" or "tidings close to God."[3] Gossip in its current modern meaning is, of course, almost the opposite—the betrayal of one's neighbor by slander.

Here is another happy thought. Think how people of different cultural and social backgrounds might learn from one another and enjoy one another's company if they gather to tell stories of human goodness in their particular culture and society. I have told mine: I have provided anecdotes and biographies. Your vignettes of goodness, your selection of exceptionally good people, will surely differ from mine. But will they all have something important in common? What might this be?

Human Goodness

1

Vignettes

Range and Variety of Goodness

An infant is a demanding tyrant, turning lobster pink in anger when thwarted. As one looks at the newborn's contorted face and kicking legs, one can't help being thankful that its power to do harm is limited. As it grows older, its tantrums may abate, but it remains—so psychologists tell us—a center of egoism, seeing the world almost wholly from the point of view of its own urgent needs.

A child two to three years old remains self-centered and gains physical strength as well as emotional range, including the emotion of jealousy when a new sibling arrives. A toddler can easily cause an infant extreme harm. The ability, the motive, and the opportunity are all there. Yet harm is very rarely done. It would appear that a two year old knows or senses that the act of harming is wrong. Psychologist Jerome Kagan puts this more positively when he identifies in human beings a desire to gain and maintain a sense of virtue. Animals other than humans, says Kagan, lack pride, shame, and guilt because the concern with right and wrong and the desire to feel virtuous are "like the appearance of milk in mammalian mothers, a unique event that was discontinuous with what was prior." In other words, "not even the cleverest ape could be conditioned to be angry upon seeing one animal steal food from another."[1]

We are used to seeing language and symbolic thought as a special creation, one that is pretty much confined to the human species. Kagan reminds us that the moral sense is another one of those "special creations," a jump in the evolutionary process. What have we made of this capacity—this gift of nature, or if you like, of God? Unlike nonhuman animal capacities, such as those of motion and the senses, all of which are more or less fully developed in the course of maturation, the capacities unique to humans—those for thinking and moral excellence—are only modestly activated unless society, under the prompting of some exceptional individual or individuals, deliberately promotes them.

"Good" as Aesthetic-Moral Appreciation

An American father calls his baby son "Folds" because he is endearingly fat. The father runs his finger over the crease at the back of his son's head to feel the skin's silken warmth and to induce in him a gurgling sound and a dimpled smile. The father's appreciation is clearly aesthetic-erotic. Not just the parent but grown-ups generally look upon the human baby as among nature's finest creations. The appeal, however, is not just aesthetic-erotic. There is also the quality of innocence—a moral quality—that touches us deeply.

In 1963 the Harris family visited me in Albuquerque, New Mexico. We decided to drive to Chaco Canyon, where there were some old Indian ruins. The drive took us many hours, and by the time we arrived at the little town of Cuba it was already dark. We checked into a motel. Helen put Anne on a small canvas chair and placed the chair on a table. Anne was about six months old. She had a delicate beauty—a full-blown female loveliness rather than mere baby cuteness. One would not dream of calling her "Folds." Anne sucked at a milk bottle, releasing the nipple from time to time to smile most charmingly at her circle of admirers. "Oops," said Helen, for she saw "water" dripping through the canvas chair onto the table. But Anne was quite unconcerned; she continued to hold court. Her total disregard for adult etiquette when nature's demands were in question aroused my admiration.

The cult of the child began in Europe in the eighteenth century. Young Mozart helped to promote the cult, for this "most famous musical prodigy in history was marked from the outset as the quintessential, perfect child. In an extraordinary series of triumphs, he was received, feted, and honored by the royal families of Europe. . . . He was kissed by empresses and patted by Marie Antoinette. And all because he was . . . the very incarnation of a miracle, one whose small body exemplified the infinite perfectibility of the child and, by inference, of mankind."[2]

Children are able to concentrate on tasks that interest them. Seeing them thus, their brows slightly furrowed as they work on a game or school lesson, can be most satisfying to grown-ups. Young Mozart showed this power of concentration to a remarkable degree. And it was not just in music; it was also there in arithmetic. When, at age three, Mozart learned how to add and subtract, he covered the table, the chairs, the walls, and even the floor in chalk figures.[3] A warm and cuddly young human, unlike other cuddly mammals, can exhibit a cool and forbidding intellect. Good! What else can one say?

> A car pulled up beside her, throwing off motor heat. The car was full of loud teenage boys. The driver, a Hispanic boy of about eighteen, wanted to make a right turn, but he was blocked by a stalled car. . . . He was banging his horn and yelling out the window; his anger was hot and all over the place. His delicate beauty was almost too bright-lit by his youth and maleness. . . . He yelled and pounded his horn. . . . It was like he was at war, like he could kill. . . . In a real war, thought Laura, he would rush into danger before the other men and be called a hero. . . .
>
> [The boy] turned in his seat to shout something to the other boys in the car. . . . He turned again and saw Laura staring at him. Their eyes met. . . . Laura crossed the street. She thought, I told him he was good. I told him with my eyes and he heard me.[4]

Laura, the character in Mary Gaitskill's story, saw male beauty and aggression. She called it good. Good, obviously, not in the usual moral sense. Good as the Behemoth is good—"the strength in his loins, the force in the navel of his belly" (Job 40:16).

Exceptional athletes move with a natural grace. "Grace," as in "graceful," is a term of aesthetic approbation. But it carries a hint of something deeper—of being in God's favor, of being in a state of grace. So George Steiner seems to have felt toward his room-mate at the University of Chicago. In exchange for helping him, Alfie, through his courses, he "would show me something I would *never* be able to match. . . . Alfie crouched on the floor, stretched both arms in front of him in absolute tautness, and leaped into the upper bunk. No Nureyev has surpassed for me the explosive arc of that leap, displaying a paratrooper's perfect command over his tensed thighs, over the hidden coil in the small of his back. I stood transfixed, close to tears at my own awkwardness and the bare beauty of that gesture."[5]

Tom Seaver left the Mets for the Cincinnati Reds. He cried when he cleared out his locker at Shea Stadium. "Our national preoccupation with the images and performances of great athletes is not a simple matter. The obsessive intensity with which we watch their beautiful movements, their careless energy, their noisy narcissistic joy in their own accomplishments is remarkably close to the emotions we feel when we observe very young children at play. . . . Off the field, Tom Seaver is not a child, of course, but an articulate and outspoken young man." At the game "our joy in him was unstinted. Yelling at the last fastball of the day, watching Tom walk off the mound after still another extraordinary pitching performance, we would rise and shout and clap our hands for his skill, for his good looks, for his sweaty, smiling joy over another famous victory. Savoring the victory, loving him, we suddenly become younger, for we had surely glimpsed ourselves out there, if only for an instant—ourselves at some glowing, youthful best."[6]

The word "beautiful" when applied to children and superb athletes hints at an inner glow—a core goodness—that is the source of their own happiness and of happiness to others who have the good fortune to see them. There is, however, another sense to "beauty," one that is tainted by the social, as in the expression "beautiful people." Malcolm Muggeridge says dismissively, "How beautiful are the bodies of the rich as they run, laughing, into the sea! Or as they sit at the wheel of a fast car, or look at one another's perfection across a white table-cloth beside the blue Mediterranean, Gatsby-like in their whiteness and fragrance and freshness!"[7] There is here none of the *sweaty,* smiling joy of a Tom Seaver.

Decency and Wholesomeness

The child and the athlete stand for health and wholesomeness. "Health," "whole," and "wholesomeness" have the same root as "holy." The idea lingers in our language that a good person has to be a whole person, not defective in some way, either physically or morally. It is a dangerous idea, of course. A person in robust health may be a monster of evil, whereas a cripple may be a saint. Still, in England and anglicized North America the association of physical robustness with courage and other moral qualities is retained in an ideal that is sometimes called "masculine Christianity." The root of the idea reaches back to medieval chivalry insofar as it is concerned with defending the weak, but to it are added such nineteenth-century virtues as self-reliance and competence.

The good man I have in mind is the poised and honorable school prefect, the big-brotherly athlete, the brave and resourceful soldier or explorer, the benign and efficient administrator. He is bright without being intellectual, self-assured enough to be thoughtless of self, principled yet tolerant, decent and kind but not driven to save the world, just a corner of it, and polite—a politeness elevated by natural grace.

E. A. Wilson and H. R. Bowers were members of Robert Falcon Scott's Antarctic expedition. It can truly be said that Wilson loved God's creation—his fellow men and nature, men both cultivated and rough-edged, and nature not only in its soothing beauties but also in its harshness. To Wilson, blizzards, hunger, and pain, too, were messages from God. Teammate Apsley Cherry-Garrard was at a loss for words to praise him. "However much of good I may write of Wilson, his many friends in England, those who served with him on the ship or in the hut, and most of all those who had the good fortune to sledge with him (for it is sledging which is far the greatest test) will be dissatisfied, for I know that I cannot do justice to his value. If you knew him you could not like him: you simply had to love him. Bill was the salt of the earth. If I were asked what quality it was before others that made him so useful, so lovable, I think I should answer that it was because he never for one moment thought of himself."

Bowers's teammates described him as utterly indifferent to hardship, as being "infernally cheerful" even under severe duress, and as having the resourcefulness to extract himself and others from the most difficult situations. Men like Bowers, wrote Cherry-Garrard, "may be at a discount in conventional life; but give me a snowy ice-floe waving about on top of a black swell, a ship thrown aback, a sledge-party almost shattered, or one that has just upset their supper on the floor cloth of the tent . . . and I will lie down and cry for Bowers to come and lead me to food and safety."[8]

In the United States Bill Hilgendorf of Yale is a good example of nature's gentleman—to use an old-fashioned term. I call him that because his qualities seem inborn, a gift rather than cultivated. A fellow student writes: "He was president of our class, respected unto veneration, a jock's jock. . . . He'd lived two floors above me in Jonathan Edwards since sophomore year, unfailingly nice when we passed on the stairs, but I was too awed to engage him much. He looked like the steel engraving of Lancelot in *Idylls of the King*, the subject of the second half of my thesis. Wisconsin-born, rock solid, Bill had no guile about him at all, and no arrogance either. Nothing to dilute the Eagle Scout mix of authority and decency. . . . I don't know how not to make him sound like a cheap paper saint. He wasn't stiff or holier-than-thou. The aura around him was a sunlit field in a winning season, but he somehow didn't consume the light himself. It always seemed to be shining back on the person he was talking to."[9]

Wilson and Bowers died with Scott in Antarctica. Their story has been told many times. Hilgendorf died in Hong Kong, falling off a mountain while still a student at Yale. They all died young, as suits heroes. It is hard to imagine them as old men, rubbing their arthritic hands in front of the fire.

But, of course, dying young is not required! It is just that the kind of goodness and wholesomeness I have in mind is the common badge of youth. Here is one more example. George Willig is a modest-mannered young *ascensioniste*. On 26 May 1977 he climbed the South Tower of the World Trade Center. At the top, the police who were there to arrest him asked for his autograph. The city first sued Willig for $250,000 and then treated him as a civic hero. Willig has an attractive wife, works at making toys, and explained that his plan had been to scale the tower a day earlier, "but I had made an appointment to give blood on Wednesday. . . . I couldn't keep on making excuses. So I arbitrarily picked today."[10]

Good Manners

Being good and having good manners are not the same thing. Being good is more deeply grounded than merely having good manners, which can be picked up easily, as from an etiquette book. Yet manners can and do segue into effortless habit, a style of being, and style, as the saying goes, is the man. When philosophers consider human goodness or morality, they seldom bother with manners. I do because without them—without an active cultivation of them—life is endless irritation and simmering conflict.

"Baudouin [a villager of the Ituri rain forest in Africa] had the nicest manners I had encountered in a long time. Once, as he walked beside me, with his hands clasped shyly in front of him, I tripped and he said, with a look of real distress, as if it were *his* fault, 'Oh, pardon, monsieur.'"[11]

"Frank [sixty-two years old] goes racing cycling and even wears lycra-shorts. He has several bikes and when someone else in his club admired one of them and offered to buy it, Frank made him a present of it. When they were out cycling next, the young man to whom he had given the bike kept just behind him, mile after mile, until Frank slowed down and waved him on, whereupon the young man streaked away into the distance far faster than Frank could go. Afterwards he asked him why it had taken him so long to pass and the young man said: 'Well, I didn't feel it was right to pass you on your own bike.'"[12]

During my graduate student years I used to crisscross the country on a Greyhound bus. At the crowded stations and on the bus itself I met Americans whom I did not normally encounter in my usual homes, which were college campuses and towns. I was struck by unexpected gallantries in the tacky environment of the Greyhound bus. When the time came to board, bewildered and insecure elderly travelers pushed their way in, commandeered the best seats, and ordered greasy-haired teenagers to put their bags on the overhead rack, which they did with a mere flip of their forearm. The teenagers might have been high school dropouts or even gang members. The bus station and traveling by bus were, however, "home" to them. They exuded confidence. This confidence and the pride they had in their strength enabled them to act like gallant knights.

I was in Panama in 1959, studying the coastline. I needed to get to a sandbar separated from the mainland by a stretch of mangrove swamp. I waited for the tide to withdraw so that I could find a path and walk over the swamp to the sandbar, a distance of a couple of hundred yards. Hours later, having completed my survey, I packed my notebooks, camera, and compass to make the return journey. To my astonishment, I found a wholly unfamiliar landscape. High tide had covered the swamp in one to two feet of water. Must I wade through this muck? A fisherman came toward me, pushing an old bike on the handlebar of which was a row of fish, which he no doubt intended to sell in the mainland village. His gestures told me that I was to sit on his bike and that he would push me through the swamp, which he did. As soon as I got off the bike I dug into my wallet for a few dollars to give him. But when I turned around he was nowhere to be seen.

On 28 December 1982 my car got stuck in a snowdrift on one of the most heavily traveled streets of Minneapolis. Through my snow-spattered window I could see a figure pushing a car across the street. When that car was freed and had roared off, the figure came to me and offered help. It turned out that he was an employee of the Towers Condominium, where I lived. We went back to the condominium's garage together. On our way I engaged him in conversation. He told me that he lived in St. Paul and that he had to abandon his own car on his way to work. He trudged two miles through the heavy snow, stopping periodically to help other drivers free their vehicles. In the garage I turned around to thank him. On the snowy street I hadn't looked at him because I had to concentrate on my driving. Now I could look, and what I saw was a young face glowing with health. He smiled to reveal a set of perfect white teeth. I couldn't help feeling that on that cold snowy day, frustrated by my inability to get to my office, I had the great good fortune to meet a child of God.

During the summer of 1990 I had lunch at Shanghai Minnie, a Chinese fast-food restaurant on University Avenue in Madison. A young couple with a baby were also eating there. When they finished the man put the paper dishes and plastic forks into the trash bin and returned the trays. The woman strapped her child into the stroller. The man opened the door for them to pass, and then, to my surprise, he returned to the table and adjusted the chairs so that they stood as neatly as they did before the family occupied them.

On a January day in 1994 the temperature plus the wind chill factor sank to a record low of -70°F. I sat at a table next to the window, having my Saturday morning breakfast at the International House of Pancakes. I saw a young woman getting into her car. A moment later she got out again, lifted the hood, and stared at the engine. Her car wouldn't start, and it was obvious she didn't know what to do. At that moment a young man came out of the restaurant and went to his car, parked next to the woman's. They chatted a while. The man opened his trunk, took out jump-start cables, and tried to attach the clamps to the batteries. He had to remove his heavy gloves to do so. After bending over the engine for twenty minutes or so, fiddling with it, it roared into life. From my window seat I saw the woman's face turn from frustration to radiant smile. Why did the man help? After all, the woman was not in serious difficulty. She could have stepped back into the warm restaurant and waited for help from a service station.

I visited China in the summer of 2005 after an absence of sixty-four years. I expected many changes, but I did not expect that some things remained the same, one of which was—to my delight—Chinese considerateness. Two students—Zhi Cheng (male) and Yi-Ou (female)—were assigned to be my guides. We visited the Great Wall in the morning and then had lunch at a place that specialized in hot buns. When they came I bit eagerly into one, which squirted delicious juice into my mouth. At this point I saw that our driver, who sat and ate quietly with us, had ordered garlic for himself. I remembered eating raw garlic with meat buns when I was a child, so I asked for some—to Zhi Cheng's surprise. He probably didn't think I was Chinese enough to have a taste for raw garlic, but he peeled a clove for me. I could have done this myself, but to have a young man, seated to my left, do it for me was unexpected luxury. When I had finished, Yi-Ou, the young woman seated to my right, handed me another clove. Fed hand to mouth by youngsters, could I ask for more? Yet there was more.

The Ming tombs were on our afternoon schedule. The drive there should have taken half an hour. Zhi Cheng used his cell phone to call his professor to report on our progress. Apparently, the professor told him that I should be given an opportunity to rest. Up to this point on our tour I had sat in the front seat next to the driver so as to get a better view. That was Zhi Cheng's idea. Now he suggested that I change seats with Yi-Ou and sit in the back, where there was more room. I did as I was told, delighted to be so pampered. Then Zhi Cheng said, "You will feel more comfortable if you lean against me and rest your head on my shoulder." His offer startled me. I yearned to accept but didn't, having lived too long in the United States.

Good Manners Beget Good Society

The Ituri villager who says, "Oh, pardon, monsieur," when his American guest trips over a tree branch on the forest floor is certainly showing good manners. So is the young cyclist who refrains from overtaking his older companion; so are the parents who clear the table at the fast-food restaurant and the father who returns to readjust the seats. All of them have been well brought up, taught to behave in a certain way by precept and example. However, when the action is demanding, as it was for the young man who helped a stranger start her car in intense cold, the behavior pushes beyond mere good manners to the edge of heroism. Can such behavior be taught? Certainly, it is not listed in any etiquette book. I shall take up undoubted heroism later, but for now I want to stay with manners because, by encouraging people to *play* at being good, manners may make people actually good; at least, such play, sincere or not, will make society itself more genial, more civilized.

Great discrepancy in power and wealth existed in seventeenth-century France. What would French society have been like without the tempering influences of courtly etiquette? Louis XIV, the Sun King, was well known for never passing a charwoman at Versailles without taking off his hat to her, and society was quick to catch on. "To Mme de Maintenon, for instance, the most glaring evidence of her sister-in-law's vulgarity is that she will accept something at table from a footman without thanking him." Good manners, however, can be exaggerated to absurdity. "St. Simon, driving back from Fontainebleau with his wife and two maids in the carriage, had the misfortune to meet the Duc de Coislin, the politest man in France, broken down on the road, and of course stopped to offer him a lift. As the exchange of preliminary compliments threatened to be interminable, St. Simon was forced to get out into the mud himself and entreat his fellow-peer to join him. Only then did Coislin discover the presence of the maids, 'the young ladies,' as he called them; he would not think of depriving them of their places: the war of compliment began all over again, in spite of St. Simon's insistence that the 'young ladies' could follow on in Coislin's coach when it had been repaired. After a long delay Coislin was tricked into entering St. Simon's coach, where

St. Simon had to hold him down to prevent him from climbing out of the window to offer a final apology to the maids."[13]

Václav Havel, former president of Czechoslovakia (now the Czech Republic), is a strong advocate of good taste and good manners. He sees them not just as social decor but as qualities that are fundamental to good governance and a humane society. "Oddly enough," Havel responded to a *Time* magazine interviewer, "I have found that good taste plays an important role in politics. Why is it like that? The most probable reason is that good taste is a visible manifestation of human sensibility toward the world. . . . I realized how important good taste was for politics. During political talks, the feeling of how and when to convey something, of how long to speak, whether to interrupt or not, the degree of attention, how to address the public, forms to be used so as not to offend someone's dignity and on the other hand to say what has to be said, all these play a major role."[14]

Communism had infused the entire society with a certain ugliness, from tasteless government offices and officious bureaucrats down to tacky restaurants and stores manned by surly waiters and salespeople. Havel considered it his duty, as the first president to be installed after the fall of communism, to use his position to preach civility, to stir the people's dormant goodwill. "People need to hear that it makes sense to behave decently or to help others, to place common interests above their own, to respect the elementary rules of human coexistence." Czechoslovakia was a poor country in the early 1990s, but that did not excuse bad manners and ugly houses and public buildings. "No one can persuade me that it takes a better-paid nurse to behave more considerately to a patient, that only an expensive house can be pleasing, that only a wealthy merchant can be courteous to his customers and display a handsome sign outside, that only a prosperous farmer can treat his livestock well. I would even go further, and say that, in many respects, improving civility of everyday life can accelerate economic development—from the culture of supply and demand, of trading and enterprise, right down to the culture of values and lifestyle."[15]

Good and Happy Society: Two Pictures

Everyone is afraid of Virginia Woolf, a sharp-tongued lady who can never be accused of sentimentality. Therefore, when she offers a picture of happy family life, we must accept it as real. She wrote in her diary: "Why all this pother about life? It can produce old Walter, bubbling & chubby; and old Lotta, stately & content; and handsome Charles, loving & affectionate. Plunge deep into Walter's life and it is all sound and satisfactory. His son kisses him and says, 'Bless you father.' He sinks back chuckling on his cushions. He chooses a macaroon. He tells a story. Lotta purrs, in her black velvet dress."[16]

Beyond the family there is the larger society, the nation, made up mostly of strangers, and yet, under certain circumstances, they are fellow countrymen and family too. Landscape itself has a part in knitting people together. Antoine de Saint-Exupéry gives this idyllic picture of an afternoon in the south of France. "It was on a day before the war, on the banks of the Saône, near Tournus. We had chosen lunch at a restaurant whose wooden terrace overlooked the river. Leaning on a plain table scarred by customers' knives, we had ordered two Pernods. . . . And since two bargemen were unloading their barge nearby, we invited them along. We had invited them quite naturally, as friends, perhaps because we felt an inner joy. It was obvious they would respond to our invitation, and we enjoyed a drink together."

The natural setting helped. "The sun was warm. Its warm honey spread over the poplar tree on the opposite bank and over the plain to the horizon. We were more and more joyful, still without really knowing why. The sun shone reassuringly, the river flowed reassuringly, the meal tasted reassuring; the bargemen who responded to our invitation and the waitress who served us smilingly, as if presiding over an eternal feast, were equally reassuring. We were completely at peace. . . . We tasted a kind of bliss where, all wishes being fulfilled, we had nothing to confide to each other."[17]

Beyond Good Manners: Going the Extra Mile

"Have a good day." In the Midwest you often hear a restaurant manager or shopkeeper say this to you as you leave. My sophisticated friends tend to dismiss it as meaningless or cheap. For my part, I consider it a mark of civilization, like other forms of greeting such as "good morning," "how are you," and "you are welcome." They are not meant to be sincere but are, rather, verbal mannerisms that smooth daily intercourse. Moreover, everything we say, no matter how slight, *has* consequence. "Have a good day" may be said perfunctorily, but I can nevertheless cash it by asking right away for street directions. My well-wisher can hardly refuse! In one of my utopian dreams I envisage a future in which politeness is carried matter-of-factly beyond words to action—even arduous action.

Here is a scenario. My car breaks down on the highway. I get out, lift the hood, and peer inside—useless gestures, for I have no idea how a car engine works. The car following mine stops. The driver comes over to help. He does so not because he knows me or feels my pain but from simple good manners. A civilization in which everyday good manners go to such an extreme is, of course, more advanced than ours. Yet, even now, there are such people.

In 1980 I was flying nonstop from Minneapolis to Boston. An hour or so after taking off we were served dinner. People leaned back from their lunch trays and relaxed over a second cup of coffee. Suddenly, a voice asked through the intercom whether there was a doctor on the plane, for one of the passengers—an elderly woman—had choked on her food and couldn't breathe. A young intern answered the call. He had the woman stretched out in the aisle. He bent over her, put his mouth over hers, and proceeded to suck out the vomit. The captain told us that we would have to make an emergency landing at Chicago's O'Hare Airport. An ambulance already stood ready on the strip when we touched down. The sick woman was taken to the hospital, accompanied by the young doctor. We waited an hour for his return. No one on board seemed irritated. No one complained of the delay. I was impressed first by the young doctor's dedication (I can't imagine myself swallowing a stranger's vomit), second by the sense of community among the passengers, and third by society's efficiency in providing the needed services. Who was the passenger? Not a VIP, just someone traveling economy class like me.

In 1995 Haiti was again in a state of near collapse, its population under siege by ruthless armed men called the Macoutes. American soldiers were sent there to restore order. At one of the worst fighting areas, a reporter who accompanied the soldiers noted: "A pick-up truck drove in. In my state of readiness [for an assault by the Macoutes], that seemed truly ominous but then I saw that the passengers riding in the back were several middle-aged white women in dresses and straw hats. 'We're do-gooders!' one of them cried cheerily as her Haitian driver helped her down from the truck. She explained that they belonged to Ventures to People, and came from West Bend, Wisconsin. 'It's community outreach through the Mothers' Club,' she said. They were there to establish an 'outreach food program' at the Mirebalais hospital."

The reporter marveled at this American compulsion to do good at home and abroad. She saw it in the soldiers in Haiti and in the young anthropologist and physician who had gone native and given his salary to his adopted compatriots, the Haitians, and she saw it in the white-haired ladies who could have stayed home to knit or play bingo. But no, they had to come and do good beyond the call of duty. And the result? At least to one reporter Mirebalais felt safer "now that the Mothers' Club was in town."[18]

From India comes this story of someone going the extra mile—no, extra many miles.

> One night, sick for weeks in a hut in Mahabalipuram in the south of India, I [anthropologist Alphonso Lingis] woke out of the fevered stupor of days to find that the paralysis that had incapacitated my arms was working its way into my chest. I stumbled out into the starless darkness of the heavy monsoon night. On the shore, gasping for air, I felt someone grasp my arm. He was naked, save for a threadbare loincloth, and all I could understand was that he was from Nepal. How he had come here, to the far south of [the] Indian subcontinent[,] . . . I had no way of learning from him. . . . He engaged in a long conversation,

unintelligible to me, with a fisherman awakened from a hut at the edge of the jungle and finally loaded me in an outrigger canoe to take me, I knew without understanding any of his words, through the monsoon seas to the hospital in Madras, sixty-five miles away. My fevered eyes contemplated his silent and expressionless face . . . as he labored in the canoe, and it was completely clear to me that should the storm become violent, he would not hesitate to save me, at the risk of his own life.

We disembarked at a fishing port where he put me first on a rickshaw and then on a bus for Madras, and then he disappeared without a word or glance at me. . . . I would never see him again.[19]

Indifference to Self-Image

Good people, however different they are from one another in personal traits, are alike in their unconcern with the self, not only the physical self (the body), which they are willing to endanger or sacrifice for a cause, but also the image of self. They don't yearn to be seen in the best light, they have no desire to stage-manage circumstance so that their life can have the rounded polish of art.

Nelson Mandela is one of the truly good men of our time. We have many reasons to admire him. But, for me, one small incident in his postprison life, overshadowed by many others that are far more important, nevertheless stands out as indisputable evidence of his goodness. One evening on Ted Koppel's TV show, *Nightline,* "for most of the two hours, Mr. Mandela was totally untelegenic," notes a reporter. "Refusing to play a role in the conventional TV illusion of an intimate chat, he scarcely glanced at Mr. Koppel during the entire first hour, instead fixing his gaze down and away and concentrating fiercely on the questions he was asked." An eight-year-old boy—Bernard—was in the audience. When the interview came to an end, "Mr. Mandela embraced Bernard, somewhat awkwardly, and waved goodbye to the crowd. But the show wasn't over. Apparently not knowing quite what to do with Bernard, Mr. Mandela offered him an autograph. Bernard was interested. Mr. Mandela asked Mr. Koppel for a piece of paper, and, when he got it, set about the business of giving Bernard an autograph, ask the spelling of his name, [Bernard O. Charles III] and so on. This was laborious, undramatic business getting seriously anticlimactic. Mr. Mandela finally finished the autograph for Bernard. He was still not playing to the camera. . . . He carefully tore the page he had signed for Bernard out of the notebook Mr. Koppel had given him, then handed the notebook back to Mr. Koppel, thanking him. These gestures were entirely natural, but because they were occurring on television, and in place of a rousing finale, they seemed very strange, almost unearthly."[20]

In Mandela's shoes I would have wanted to end the interview with a noble peroration against racism, and this is because I see life as theater and myself as playwright and hero in a drama that ends with a flourish, bringing down the curtain to the sound of applause. I am, in other words, more Oscar Wilde than Nelson Mandela. "The day after Oscar Wilde told [the story "The Happy Prince"] half a dozen of the 'cicadas' [Wilde's young admirers] went down to the station to see him off. They clustered round his carriage window as he kept up a stream of epigrams, timed to culminate as the train drew out of the station. But something went wrong, and the train, having started[,] backed in again. The students were still on the platform, but Wilde, rather than risk anticlimax, closed his window and remained absorbed in his paper until the train drew out again."[21]

Unworldliness

Archbishop William Temple had a guest. He said to him, "Please take a chair, Mr. Jones," whereupon the guest stood up to his full height and said, "Mr. *Montague*-Jones, if you please," to which the archbishop responded, "Oh, in that case, take two chairs!"

I appreciate the archbishop's quick wit, but I identify with Mr. Jones. We—most of us—are, alas, as vain and solicitous of our position in society as he was. But what of Temple? In the British hierarchy he, as the archbishop of Canterbury, ranked above the prime minister, and his place of residence was a palace—the Lambeth Palace. Yet, apparently, one could live in a palace and still be unworldly. The following story was told of Temple and his friend, the noted economic historian R. H. (Harry) Tawney. The two met at a house in Mecklenburg Square to talk of eternal things and had been doing so for some hours, until Harry asked William whether he was ready for supper. William said that he was but "wondered how it was going to be provided; he had seen no sign that it was in preparation. But Harry now went up to a stack of bookshelves and began to rummage behind one shelf of books after another. William watched to see what was coming, and what eventually came out of its lair was a brace of cold mutton chops."

After dining, these two friends went on talking till it was time to go to bed. William's bed? It was to be the wooden bench that ran around the inside of a bow window. In the small hours of the night, William awoke with a start. "What had roused him was that the light from the street had doubled in intensity. Looking up, he saw a policeman's lantern trained on his face, and behind the lantern, he saw a policeman's face looking down at the sleeper dubiously." The archbishop told this tale with a mixture of amusement and affection to Arnold Toynbee.[22]

Alexander Grothendieck turned down his share ($135,000) of the prestigious Crafoord Prize of the Royal Swedish Academy of the Sciences, an award introduced in 1982 for scientists working in disciplines not covered by the Nobel Prize. Why? Well, Grothendieck said he had no need of the prize money, since his professor's salary was already "much more than sufficient for the material needs of myself and those I am responsible for." Moreover, he believed the decisive test for the fertility of ideas was the test of time. "Fertility is recognized by its offspring, and not by honors."[23]

Selflessness

Mother love is selfless. It has the force of nature, says John Updike somewhere, comparing it to the way water forces its way out of a bottle when it turns into ice. Comparing mother love to water and ice is, to say the least, unusual, but I think Updike is after the idea of the inevitability of a physical law. Father love is, by comparison, more human. Hugh MacDiarmid, in a poem, notes that while he loves his little son, he could not confine himself to the child's bedside when he was ill. He grew impatient of the child's "squalid little needs" and longed for the large, bustling world outside. Yet the child's mother had no trouble attending to "the dread level" of nothing but life itself and stayed with the child until he recovered.

In talking about human goodness (and selflessness, in particular) I have eschewed examples from the most obvious source—motherhood—for two reasons. First, I want instances where goodness does not benefit the "doer of good" in the biological/evolutionary sense. Second, I believe, like Iris Murdoch, that "mothers have many egoistic satisfactions and much power." She suggests that "the aunt may be the selfless unrewarded doer of good. I have known such aunts. In the activity of such workers [besides aunts, nurses, social workers, parish priests, the dedicated schoolteacher], egoism has disappeared unobtrusively into the care and service of others."[24]

Selflessness of a heroic and rather showy kind, wholly admirable nevertheless, is perhaps more common among men. Consider this report by F. A. Worsley, a member of Sir Ernest Shackleton's polar expedition. Shackleton and his crew never were able to cross the Antarctic continent as they had intended. For one reason and another they had to turn back. The last stage of the trip back necessitated the crossing of eight hundred miles of storm-tossed icy sea between Elephant Island, at the tip of the Antarctic continent, and South Georgia. Three of the strongest members of the team were to leave Elephant Island at noon on 24 April 1916. Right at the start they encountered near disaster. "As we launched the *James Caird* she fell over in the surf, and threw McNeish and Vincent overboard. McCarthy and I stretched out oars and held them up, pushing them towards the men on the shore, who pulled them to safety. Some of the shore party generously changed clothes with the drenched men so that the latter might start in dry condition. Only those who have visited the Polar regions can appreciate the fineness of this action, for to get into dripping clothes in such circumstances is almost a martyrdom. Moreover, the men who put on those wet garments knew that it would be many a day before they were dry again. Actually, it was a fortnight."[25]

Gratitude and Obligation

"Gratitude is heaven itself," said William Blake. If so, why is it so rare? The answer is that in ordinary life we almost never think how much we owe to nature and society. On rare occasions we may feel grateful for the morning sun pouring into and brightening our kitchen, the postman's friendly smile, children's laughter, the sound of a late Beethoven quartet coming out of the radio, the responsive, barely audible hum of our car when we turn the key, the fragrance of freshly baked pie, the first sip of coffee at our favorite café, the clean and cool bedsheets that welcome us at night, and so on. The list, once we start making one up, is interminable, all the more so when we begin to consider our indebtedness to the labor, thought, and imagination of all those who have preceded us. Each of us might ask, "With so much given, what do I contribute in return? What have I added to the wealth of creation?" It is a humbling thought, for the answer must be, "very little."

Thoughtlessness makes us ungrateful. We may also wish to repress the feeling of gratitude because it obliges us to forget not only the ills that have come our way but also the pleasure of nursing them in righteous indignation. Gratitude wells up naturally in a truly good person—a saint. And there are few of them.

Teresa of Ávila was a saint, grateful for the smallest favor that came her way. Why, she said, she could be bought with a sardine. That sounded just right. If she had said that she was grateful to God for offering up his own son for her salvation, well, that might be theologically correct, but it would have sounded pretentious. A good person—a humble person—needed only a sardine from God to feel grateful.

Gratitude, being heaven itself, motivates us to do good. When properly expressed, it also motivates the person to whom we owe gratitude to continue to do good. For this reason, "ingratitude, which constantly robs us of our enthusiasm, is one of the worst powers of evil in the world," said Albert Schweitzer. Of the ten lepers Jesus healed, only one came back to thank him. "Were the other nine ungrateful? By no means! They may even have thought of him as warmly as did the other one and spoke of what he had done for them with deep emotion. But after they had shown themselves to the priests in Jerusalem [as Jesus had told them to] and were able to go home, only one thought of returning to the lord. The others went off to their villages. They forgot the obvious thing: expressing their thanks. We, too, do the same thing hundreds and hundreds of times, in matters both great and small."[26]

Schweitzer himself regretted that he had not shown more gratitude. "When I look back at my youth, I am moved by the thought of how many people I have to thank for what they were to me and what they gave me. At the same time, however, I become depressed when I realize how little I have expressed my gratitude to those people when I was young. How many of them said farewell to life without my having told them what their kindness or patience had meant to me. Deeply moved I sometimes softly spoke at their graves the words that I should have said to them while they were living."[27]

No one to thank? Dorothy Day said that one difference between her husband, Forster, and her was this. "I felt thankful when I met Forster and fell in love with him, and he fell in love with me. I wanted to express my thanks. I told him that—how grateful I felt to be with him. He was glad to hear of my affection and gratitude, but he had no sense of there being anyone to thank. That was the point of our eventual disagreement, our separation. It wasn't something we could really argue over. . . . If a person wants to pour out her gratitude to the universe, and someone else has no desire to do that and finds such a desire foolish or absurd, then there is going to be a reckoning."[28]

In a diary entry during 1906, Tolstoy angrily noted: "People write pompously in books that when there are rights, there are also obligations. What audacious nonsense—what lies. Man has only obligations. MAN HAS ONLY OBLIGATIONS!"[29] Was this an instance of noblesse oblige—Tolstoy's feeling that because he had been given so much (talent, wealth, status), much—indeed, everything—was expected of him? Probably so, but there was more to it than that, for Tolstoy seemed to say that not just he but every person was under obligation. From a religious point of view we are all obliged to do good because we are all born noble, children of God, like Tolstoy, and we all enjoy the wealth (air, fire, water, earth) that is God's creation. Christian missionaries often say that because Christ died for their sins they are obliged to do good, including preaching the Gospel to the heathens. Maybe so. But I personally find that kind of talk bloated. I much prefer Teresa of Ávila's motivation. It was gratitude for a sardine. Or Albert Schweitzer's motivation. It was gratitude for happiness.

"An uncomfortable doctrine prompts me in whispered words. You are happy, it says. Therefore you are called to give much. Whatever you have received more than others in health, in talents, in ability, in success, in a pleasant childhood, in harmonious conditions of home life, all this you must not take to yourself as a matter of course. You must pay a price for it. You must render in return an unusually great sacrifice of your life for other life."[30] So wrote Schweitzer. He would have found a kindred spirit in William James, who spoke of "the sentiment of honor" rather than obligation. "The sentiment of honor is a very penetrating thing. When you and I, for instance, realize how many innocent beasts have had to suffer in cattle-cars and slaughter-pens and lay down their lives that we might grow up, all fattened and clad, to sit together here in comfort and carry on this discourse, it does, indeed, put our relation to the universe in a more solemn light. Are we not bound to take some suffering upon ourselves, to do some self-denying service with our lives, in return for all those lives upon which ours are built?"[31]

John Cowper Powys, for his part, directed his gratitude to all the humans who preceded him and who contributed to making his life secure and comfortable. "There is an awareness that has been the accompaniment of all my days; namely an intense realization of the privilege of having a roof over my head, a blanket over my bed, dry boots on my feet, a good fire to warm my shins, and a dish of bread and milk in front of me! Never have I taken for granted the inestimable privilege of being assured of the necessities of life. It is the one point where I drop my touchy individualism and grow humanly and most humbly thankful. I feel grateful not only to Chance, but to the actual human race, whose 'collective' activities in this great twenty-five thousand years 'Plan' of theirs, have given me protection from these elements I am always praising so!"[32]

Gratitude is pure self-indulgence if it is just a warm feeling. To be real, action must follow. Here is a story from Auschwitz that shows gratitude taking the form of heroic action. An SS guard named Viktor Pestek approaches various inmates with an offer to help them escape. His plan is to get hold of another officer's uniform and put the uniform on an inmate; the two of them will then leave the camp together. The ruse succeeds, but eventually Pestek is caught and executed. "Why did he take such risks? It seems that while fighting on the Russian front he had taken part in a punitive action against a village suspected of concealing resistant fighters. Pestek was wounded during the attack and left behind by his comrades. The following day several members of a Russian family found him hiding in their barn. Pestek was thirsty; instead of finishing him off, they led him to the stream."[33] Pestek never forgot this encounter with mercy. Considering the massacre that he and his comrades had just perpetrated, the surviving villagers had every reason to kill him.

Allow me one more take on gratitude. We can be grateful for many things. Come Thanksgiving and Christmas, Americans are grateful for family and friends, turkey dinners and carol singing. Tolstoy would understand, for his novels include many glowing accounts of comparable domestic felicities in Russia. But he also urges us to be grateful for something more elemental, the air, water, fire, and earth that make up nature. But I think there is something even more basic, namely, chance, the happy chance that gives rise to existence. Everything that exists seems to me gratuitous—miraculous. Our own universe, which is just one among many, according to the latest theory, is a product of chance, implausibly constituted so as to favor nebulas and stars and life. Life in the universe is, however, extremely rare. Complex forms of life are rarer still. Even on the exceptionally favored planet Earth, it took a very long time—three billion years—for evolution to produce primitive multicellular organisms. Nothing in the nature of things guaranteed that evolution would continue to produce ever more complex forms. Yet it did until, somehow, dinosaurs appeared. They lorded over the Earth. Their domination could seem permanent, but it was not to be. A cosmic event—a shower of meteors?—wiped out the dinosaurs, one consequence of which was that the surviving organisms could radiate adaptively, a process that led eventually to mammals and—yes— to us.

From the existence of the human species, my thought turns to my own existence, which is, of course, a statistical fluke. Of the millions of spermatozoa that entered my mother's womb, only one succeeded in beating out all the others to fertilize the egg and produce me. My natural feeling of gratitude for that little swimmer's prowess is, however, shadowed by guilt, for I can't help thinking that, had another spermatozoon reached the target ahead of the one that gave rise to me, the world could have had another Confucius! That I exist—that I was born rather than another— places an obligation on me to be more a comfort to than a blight on the lives of my fellow creatures.

Humility and Pride

Humility is the trickiest virtue to establish as genuine. Is self-denigration humility, or is it just another way of boasting? Is courtesy humility? When Mme de Maintenon insisted that the waiter serving her and other ladies be duly thanked each time he presented them with a leg of lamb, was she acknowledging their common humanity, or was she merely showing off her exquisite manners? For true humility, what about the retirees of Florida who appear content to play endless rounds of bingo and golf? Isn't asking so little of themselves, expecting so little of themselves, thinking so little of themselves true humility? If so, however, saints, with their high ambition, are not at all humble. Mother Teresa urged her followers "to aim very high, not to be like Abraham or David or any of the saints, but to be like our heavenly Father."[34] She is here echoing another saint, Heinrich Suso (1295–1366), who wrote: "God has not called his servants to a mediocre, ordinary life, but rather to the perfection of sublime holiness, since he said to his disciples, 'Be ye perfect as your heavenly Father is perfect.'"[35] Saint Augustine in his Soliloquia (II, 1) asks himself the question, "When you have learned that you are immortal—will that be enough for you?" To which he gives the remarkable answer: "It will be something great; but it is too little for me."[36]

In Christian thought, we are made in the image of God and rank only a little lower than the angels. It is false humility to be content to while away our time playing golf at the country club and bingo in the retirement home, to resign ourselves, in one way or another, to be "little people." Now, Nelson Mandela is demonstrably humble—a saint in politics and in sociopolitical action. Yet in his inaugural address of 1994, he says: "Our deepest fear is not that we are inadequate. Our deepest fear is that we are powerful beyond measure. It is our light, not our darkness, that most frightens us. We ask ourselves, 'Who am I to be brilliant, gorgeous, talented, fabulous?' Actually, who are you not to be? You are a child of God. Your playing small does not serve the world."

Albert Einstein rejoiced in the feeling of his utter insignificance. He put it this way: "10 December 1931. Never before have I lived through a storm like the one this night. . . . The sea has a look of indescribable grandeur, especially when the sun falls on it. . . . One feels as if one is dissolved and merged into Nature. Even more than usual, one feels the insignificance of the individual, and it makes me happy." Confronted by the majesty of nature, many of us can feel insignificant, though not so many can feel happy about it, and still fewer conclude that their life's achievements are also insignificant. Here again Einstein shows his humility. On 27 December 1949 he wrote: "It is really a puzzle what drives one to take one's work so devilishly seriously. For whom? For oneself?—one soon leaves, after all. For one's contemporaries? For posterity? No, it remains a puzzle."[37]

There is something to the notion that scientists are humble. They have to submit, after all, to the test of reality, and reality is a hard taskmaster who repeatedly humbles scientists by requiring them to start over again—and again. Scientists—or anyone who respects science—are also keenly aware that God is not an entity to be appealed to whenever bad things happen or whenever reality seems incomprehensible. In the Middle Ages, seekers after God humbled and disciplined themselves with the hair shirt. In our time, seekers after God or Truth have their own hair shirts to wear: these shirts are the hard conclusions of science, conclusions that do not offer us solace, do not make us feel important, that say we are perhaps more monkey than angel.

The noted psychologist B. F. Skinner is widely known as a hard-nosed behavioral scientist, but I would argue that being hard-nosed is his way of telling us to be more humble. Let me explain. Most people like to see themselves as free, creators as God is creator. Skinner, by contrast, sees people as essentially the play-things of genetics and environment. His is the scientific attitude. But Skinner reminds us that this scientific attitude is also "an act of self-denial that would have been understood by Thomas à Kempis." He quotes Luke 17:33: "Whoever seeks to gain his life will lose it, but whoever loses his life will preserve it," and goes on to say that this idea, congenial to science, is embraced "in mundane philosophy (Schopenhauer's annihilation of the will as the way to freedom) and literature (Conrad's Secret Sharer learning that true self-possession comes from self-abandonment)." And "it is, of course, a strong theme in Eastern mysticism." Skinner was interviewed upon the publication of his autobiography. He concluded the interview with the humble remark: "If I am right about human behavior, I have written the autobiography of a nonperson."[38]

Mother Teresa died in the shadow of Diana, Princess of Wales. "It was as if the eighty-seven-year-old nun had been waiting for the moment when she would attract the least attention, on the day before the most riveting funeral in decades." When the dying Mother Teresa heard the news of Diana's death, she reportedly said: "She died so young. I don't know the ways of God."[39]

We rarely consider the good things that come our way as unjust. By contrast, the bad things that happen to us are almost always deemed unjust—even an outrage. In other words, we all have a sense of entitlement, though not, of course, to the same degree. Consider the very different responses of two young southern women to AIDS. Belinda Mason, a journalist from Kentucky, contracted the disease from a contaminated transfusion at the time of the birth of her second child in 1987. "Though she was infected by lapses of health-care workers, she says she is not angry at them. She does not want widespread compulsory testing of them, nor does she want people with AIDS to be barred from entering the country." She plans on spending her time and energy to help people with AIDS who have been stigmatized by it. She doesn't understand bitterness. "It seems to me that it's based on an assumption [that bad things do not happen to me]. But the question is, why should it happen to anybody? I never felt I was a member of an exclusive club that should go through life unscathed." The other young woman, Kimberly Bergalis, was apparently infected by her Florida dentist. To this misfortune she responded by angrily demanding compulsory testing of all health-care workers, telling the doctors of the Florida Health Department in a letter: "I blame every single one of you bastards."[40]

Can a president be humble? It doesn't seem likely, yet history judges Abraham Lincoln to have been a humble man. Saints, we know, can be hugely ambitious and yet humble; I have given Heinrich Suso and Mother Teresa as examples. Lincoln may be added to the list. He would be the first to admit that he was greatly ambitious. His ambition, however, was to do good, to leave his country a somewhat better place than he found it; he also hoped that he himself might become a better man—a better man rather than a wiser one, for to aim to be wise was to aim too high.

Lincoln's temperament, which was disposed toward melancholy, his outlook on life, which inclined toward the darker side,
his experience of suffering and sensitivity to suffering in others all
gave him a willingness to face reality, including the reality of his
own deficiencies, and to withhold judgment on matters large and
small, even if this meant living a little longer in a state of stressful
tension. Such personality traits are common enough in a humble
person. They can lead to passivity, a state Lincoln could ill afford
in his public life and that he successfully combated.

The commemoration of dead soldiers at Gettysburg unexpectedly showcased Lincoln's modest sense of self. He was invited to
attend, but not as the principal speaker. Edward Everett, former
senator and Harvard president, was. Everett spoke with com-
manding eloquence for two hours. Lincoln followed with a speech
of three minutes, so short that it was over before the audience had
comfortably settled down in their seats. Moreover, the speech famously denigrated itself, pointing to its insignificance compared
with the events it commemorated. The irony is that today more
people know what Lincoln said than what the soldiers did.

Numerous stories and anecdotes grew around Lincoln, several
of which concerned his humility. Here is one. A man told the
president of Secretary of War Edwin McMasters Stanton's having
said angrily that in a recent decision Lincoln had acted the fool.

The teller presumably expected an explosion. Instead, Lincoln remarked thoughtfully that if Mr. Stanton had said that, then he was probably right, since he generally was.[41]

Generosity

Some people are generous by nature. I can't help thinking so by observing young children. Most seem to me possessive, reluctant to share their toys with others or willing to do so only on the basis of exchange. Parents encourage generosity in their children but within limits, for they recognize that it can bear a high cost. In 1957 I knew a remarkable boy two to three years old, the son of a colleague at Indiana University. As soon as I sat down in the family's living room, he would come to my side with a book, which he wanted me to read to him. On one occasion he brought me not a book but a toy, and then more and more toys until they piled up around me. We played with them. His mother came by from time to time to watch, and then she surprised me by teasing her son in a way that I thought put too heavy a burden on his young shoulders. She said, "Brad, are you giving all these toys to Mr. Tuan?" Her son nodded. "Really? If you do, he will take them with him when he leaves." To my surprise—and probably to his mother's too—the boy nodded again. It was Brad's bedtime. We hugged good-night. I imagine him coming downstairs the next morning and finding all his toys still there—but with one extra, the one I brought him. Is this a lesson the child learns and will stay with him as he gets older—that the more he gives the more he will receive?

The poor are privileged. Their proximity to death "matures a radical and wonderful piety, constituted in the actual life of the poor and consisting of the intense humility of the poor about their own existence as human beings. As the Ninth Psalm says, among the poor, men know that they are but men." William Stringfellow, a lawyer and Episcopalian of privileged background, spent time helping juveniles in Harlem. "I had gone out in the afternoon when it was warmer, dressed only in a shirt, chinos, and sneakers, but now that the weather had changed, I was shivering from the cold. About two blocks from my tenement, a boy I knew, who had been loafing on the corner, called out that he wanted to ask me something. As we talked he saw that I was freezing to death and so he took off his jacket and gave it to me to wear. The boy is an addict and I happened to know that the clothes on his back were virtually the only ones he had. . . . Sometimes, when his clothes were being laundered, he would have to stay in the house because he had nothing else to wear. . . . But he saw that I was cold and gave me his jacket. That is what is known as a sacrament."[42]

In his book *Arabian Sands* Wilfred Thesiger tells several stories of the extraordinary generosity of extremely poor Bedouin. One of his companions, Bin Kabina, a boy almost destitute, gives away first his loincloth and then his shirt simply because a man even poorer than himself has asked for them.

> "God, why did you do that when you have only a rag to wear?"
> "He asked me for it."
> "Damn the man. I gave him a handsome present. Really you are a fool."
> "Would you have me refuse him when he asked for it?"[43]

The boy gave simply because he was asked. He would have endorsed William James's notion of "concrete claims." "Take any demand," James wrote, "however slight, which any creature, however weak, may make. Ought it not, for its own sole sake, to be satisfied? If not, prove why not."[44]

I have repeatedly failed to rise to James's challenge. Every day I walk by two panhandlers located at the junction of Lake and State streets, one on each side, so that avoiding them is difficult. I don't put anything into their plastic cups, and this makes me feel bad. Why not give them something then? Well, if I do I shall quickly exhaust my income from Social Security and my retirement pension, for I encounter these panhandlers at least four times a day every day of the week. Another reason is that I prefer impersonal giving so as not to humiliate the recipient. That may well be just a high-minded excuse, but I am hardly the first to use it. Avoiding the panhandler in fact puts me in good company. Consider how

Immanuel Kant dealt with the problem. He was in the habit of taking his daily walk through the streets of Königsberg at exactly the same hour every day and made a point of giving money to panhandlers. "For this purpose he brought new coins with him, so as not to insult the panhandlers by giving them shabby, worn-out pieces of money. He also used to give about three times as much as was common." So far so good, until, of course, he was beleaguered by panhandlers. "He finally had to change the hour of his daily walk but was too ashamed of himself to tell the truth and invented some butcher's apprentice who, he said, had assaulted him."[45]

Kant's dilemma is familiar to all of us, though perhaps our conscience is less bothered. On the streets of American cities, we habitually walk by people, finding it convenient to ignore rather than help them. But "when we raise our convenience up to an idol—when we insist that we can't stand to even see vagrants, loiterers, and panhandlers—we make an assertion of our right to be comfortable which is as militant, as radical, as Mother Teresa's assertion of her duty to administer comfort."[46]

Simone Weil lived on the edge of poverty. What she had earned she freely gave to those in greater need. She said to Antonio, a Spaniard incarcerated in a Vichy camp whose sad situation she knew only through hearsay: "I have sent you a money order; I will send you money orders from time to time according to your needs and my possibilities. I don't think you should have any scruples or hesitation on this matter. When I have a little money in my hands, I never have the impression that this money belongs to me. It just happens to be there. And if I send it to you, I don't get the feeling that I have given it away. It simply passes from my hands to those of someone who needs it, and I have the feeling that I am not at all involved. I would really prefer that money was like water and that it flowed off by itself whenever there was a little too much of it."[47]

Paul Erdös was a brilliant mathematician who wrote in excess of 1,500 papers, books, and articles, more than any other mathematician who ever lived. He had no regular academic job, no permanent residence (he moved from campus to campus and bivouacked with his friends), and little money. But whatever money he had, he shared. "If he heard of a graduate student who needed money to continue his studies, he would send a check. Whenever he lectured in Madras he would send his fee to the needy widow of the great Indian mathematician Srinivasa Ramanujan; he had never met Ramanujan or his wife, but the beauty of Ramanujan's equations had inspired him as a young mathematician." Given his generosity, his honesty, his support of the rights of the individual, his otherworldliness, Erdös was often called a saint without the slightest tint of irony. He was, however, a saint absent religion as well as a saint with a sense of humor. He taught for a time at the

University of Notre Dame, and, despite his being an atheist (or, rather, a Platonist), he felt at home there. Only one thing bothered him. "There are too many plus signs."[48]

Giving is always, in some sense, the giving of one's life. Money is life, possessions are life (they certainly support life), time is life, and the time that is given to another can never be recovered; for that reason alone, the giving of time is among the most generous of gifts. Another gift—only possible in our advanced scientific age—is the gift of vital parts of our own body. Michael Carter was a middle school student who constantly fidgeted with his baggy pants, to the annoyance of his teacher Jane Smith. She asked him to stop. He replied that he couldn't help fidgeting, that he suffered from a kidney disease, that he was on dialysis and waiting for a kidney transplant. Ms. Smith said: "Well, I have two. Do you want one?" The story of the transplant quickly caught the country's attention, in part because Michael is black and Ms. Smith is white. Ms. Smith couldn't understand what all the fuss in the media was about. It seemed to her the natural thing to do. Michael's mother was overwhelmed with gratitude. She thanked the Lord for "that lady," for "Jane Smith." She said she was getting bold, even tough, with the Lord. "Don't you ever let her want for anything, Lord. Don't even let her want for a Kleenex."[49]

Small gifts really tend to be loans. One expects something back. But when the gift is huge, something like one's own kidney, the question of return doesn't arise. Michael's mother knows that. More interesting psychologically is that organ donors seldom feel that they are doing anything heroic or even unusual. They give not because society expects them to or because of some abstract moral ideal but because they feel—the moment they hear of the need—that they have no choice.

Generosity is not just the giving of things, time, and service. It is also how we think of another person, including the merit of his or her work. I find the personality of Charles Darwin appealing because, unlike his clever friend Thomas Huxley, whose instinct upon seeing a new book was to attack, to break (as it were) its spine, Darwin's first reading of almost any book was sympathetic. His critical intellect became seriously engaged only during the second reading. This temperamental tendency, Darwin thought, enabled him to benefit even from second-rate books. I have the feeling that Darwin could learn from the babble of a chimpanzee or a child, whereas his smart friend, ever eager to find fault, might miss an opportunity to learn from a Solomon.[50]

William James is noted for his generosity of spirit. "He seemed to me to have too high an opinion of everything," wrote John Jay Chapman, his biographer. "The last book he had read was always a 'great book'; the last person he had talked with, a wonderful being."[51]

John Bayley says of Iris Murdoch that her "awareness of others is transcendental rather than physical. She communes with their higher being, as an angel might, and is unconcerned with their physical existence, their sweaty selves." And, "for Iris, everyone she met was, so to speak, a hero, until they gave very definite signs of proof to the contrary. I have never met any one less naturally critical or censorious."[52]

Generosity is a quality C. S. Lewis had in abundance, and it shows in his literary criticism. Criticism may not even be the right word, for he chooses not to waste time attacking, preferring instead to praise with the aim of rescuing excellences that might otherwise be overlooked. However, his generosity can be excessive, according to A. N. Wilson, and so mislead the reader. An example is Lewis's expounding of John Lydgate's *The Falle of Princis,* written between 1430 and 1438. He quotes the lovely lines "And as I stoode my self alloone upon the Nuwe Yeare night, / I prayed unto the frosty moone, with her pale light," forgetting to tell the reader that the bulk of the book is dull almost beyond bearing.[53]

Don't forget Homer, the father of Western literature. His works glow because, however grimly and realistically they may portray life on the battlefield, their overall effect is one of wholesomeness that comes, ultimately, from a love of—and a generosity toward—the world. As the rhetor Dio of Prusa put it, "Homer praised almost everything—animals and plants, water and earth, weapons and horses. He passed over nothing without somehow honoring and glorifying it. Even the one man whom he abused, Thersites, he called a clear-voiced speaker." From the evidence of his works, I would say that he was a good person, a just person.

Devotion to truth can make one effortlessly generous. So it seemed with Bertrand Russell. Devastated by Wittgenstein's criticism of his work, Russell nevertheless could rejoice when he heard that Wittgenstein's work was going well. He wrote to Lady Ottoline Morrell: "You can hardly believe what a load this lifts off my spirits—it makes me feel almost young and gay."[54]

The New Testament records the following story: "Jesus sat near the temple treasury and watched the people as they dropped their money. Many rich men dropped a lot of money. A poor widow came and dropped in two copper coins, worth about a penny. He called his disciples together and said to them, 'I tell you that this poor widow put more in the offering box than all the others. For the others put in what they had to spare of their riches; but she, poor as she is, put in all she had—she gave all she had to live on'" (Mark 12:41–44).

What is exhilarating in this story and in the Thesiger story about the Arab boy is the magnificence of spirit. Supreme artistic performance can produce a similar effect. When I watch Nureyev leap into the air, I feel he has mustered all the vitality of his body, all his training and skill, all his devotion to the art of ballet to produce that one movement of supreme feline power and elegance. Even more do I feel this total giving of self, as do many others, in the singing of Maria Callas. Each time I listen to her, it is as though I were attending her one and only performance or her last performance. Conserving her voice for another day seems an alien—or, rather, an unworthy—idea to her. A poem by Edna St. Vincent Millay, used by John Ardoin in his book *The Callas Legacy,* captures Callas's spirit. In the poem Millay speaks of burning her candle at both ends. It will not last the night, "But, ah, my foes, and oh, my friends / It gives a lovely light."

With artistic performance, this total giving is almost always an intended illusion. That's why the acts of the poor widow and of the Arab boy have greater merit, at least in the eyes of God.

Respect for Animals

Saints identify with the lowly, but do the lowly include animals? Our attitude toward them is profoundly hypocritical. We deny our cruelty by keeping slaughterhouses out of sight, and we deny it with thick layers of sentiment. In modern times, only one group of people seems to me to rise above both. They are the naturalists, people who show genuine appreciation for all living things and seek to understand them by patient observation.

But what about Hindus, Buddhists, and Jains? Aren't they famous for their dedicated avoidance of doing any harm to living creatures? They were and are indeed so dedicated, but their motives are questionable. Before the sixth century BCE they avoided eating animals because they feared that animals might retaliate in the afterworld. Only later did the doctrine of reincarnation take over, and animals were not eaten because Hindus, Buddhists, and Jains believed that they themselves might be reborn as animals.[55] The motivation, in other words, is driven by human fears and concerns and not by love of animals and respect for their dignity as sentient beings. Naturally, there are exceptions. A story in the Jātaka relates that Gautama, the Buddha, saw a starving tiger and, "though composed in mind[,] was shaken with compassion by the sufferings of his fellow-creature as Mount Meru by an earthquake."[56]

In premodern Europe, Francis of Assisi was the outstanding lover of nature. All creatures, even the lowliest, were his brothers and sisters. It wasn't difficult to sing the praises of the bird, for Christianity, long before Francis, regarded birds, which have two legs like humans and wings like angels, to be creatures out of paradise. But the worm? The story was told of Francis striding along through his beloved woods, noticing a worm on the path and placing it tenderly amid the vegetation by the wayside. When he did so, "he was very far from thinking in terms of the sentimental secularism that has appropriated to itself the ancient and honorable title of humanism. To him it was self-evident that animals possessed rights, notably the Divine dispensation of life." What about reptiles and other crawling things—members of the Amphibia? Of them, even the great taxonomist Linnaeus couldn't avoid using words such as "foul," "abhorrent," "filthy," "calculating," "harsh," and "smelly." Opined Linnaeus: "God mercifully did not make many of them." And Francis of Assisi? He would no more have dreamed of spurning them than he would have lepers.[57]

Abraham Lincoln, widely known for his compassion toward his fellow countrymen, is less widely known for his compassion toward animals. He showed it even as a child. He chided his boyhood companions for their careless cruelty and argued that "an ant's life was to it, as sweet as ours to us." He retained this sensitivity into adulthood. The story is told of one time, in 1839, when he was riding to Springfield, Illinois, with a large group. They rode two by two. Lincoln rode alongside John Hardin. The group paused to water their horses. After a while Hardin came up. The others asked him where Lincoln was. "Oh," Hardin said, "when I saw him last, he had caught two little birds in his hand, which the wind had blown from their nest, and he was hunting for the nest." When Lincoln finally joined the group, some of the men laughed at him. "I could not have slept tonight," he told them earnestly, "if I had not given those two little birds to their mother."[58]

Albert Schweitzer seems to have fallen out of favor, but he remains one of my heroes if only for one thing: his impassioned plea to extend fellow feeling to all living beings. "As far back as I can remember," Schweitzer wrote, "I have suffered because of the misery I saw in the world. Already before I started school it seemed quite incomprehensible to me that my evening prayers were supposed to be limited to human beings. Therefore, when my mother had prayed with me and kissed me goodnight, I secretly added another prayer which I had made up myself for all living beings. It went like this: 'Dear God, protect and bless all beings that breathe, keep all evil from them, and let them sleep in peace.'"59

When Schweitzer escorted Adlai Stevenson, a former governor of Illinois and presidential candidate, on a tour of the hospital grounds at Lambaréné in Gabon, Stevenson noticed a large mosquito alighting on the good doctor's arm and promptly swatted it. "You shouldn't have done that," the doctor said sharply. "That was my mosquito. Besides, it wasn't necessary to call out the Sixth Fleet to deal with him."60

In the summer of 1995 I was holidaying with my brother and sister-in-law in Colorado, enjoying the splendid mountain scenery, but what remained with me as a permanent feature of my store of mental images was not the scenery but rather something I witnessed by chance. I stood in the parking lot of the Colorado School of Mines, waiting for my brother to consult with the school's information director. A man came out of an office building carrying a glass jar with a piece of cardboard laid on top. A wasp was dashing around in the jar. The man removed the cardboard and waited. The wasp failed to escape. He returned to the building but came back a few minutes later. This time he saw that the wasp had found the opening and escaped. He picked up the jar and went back to work. The man did not know he was being watched and probably would not have made much of it if he did. Puzzling is why an action so trifling could seem to me to rank with the grandeur of the Rockies.

Caring for and Respecting People

In the early days, Mother Teresa walked carefully through the slums of Calcutta. During the monsoon rains the streets would be covered with slushy, stinking garbage that oozed out of the flooded sewers. She encountered adults with plague, leprosy, and cholera, children with meningitis, and infants with diarrhea. Tuberculosis was everywhere, and it would have been difficult for her to avoid sufferers coughing up blood-flecked sputum. She embraced them all and helped everyone she encountered, even if this meant—small woman that she was—carrying the sick and dying to the hospice herself.

How could she do it? She had faith. No matter how humbly she lived, she was rich beyond measure in faith and in the joy and self-confidence that that faith gave her. She was able to overcome her natural repugnance because she was not handling sick bodies and filthy clothes, she was handling, as she herself put it, "Christ, the most beautiful one among the sons of men."

I doubt Mother Teresa read Flaubert's story "The Legend of St. Julian the Hospitaller," which she would have appreciated. Saint Julian encountered a leper.

> The leper groaned. His teeth showed at the corners of his mouth, a faster rattle shook his chest, and as each breath was taken his body hollowed to the backbone. Then he shut his eyes. "It is like ice in my bones! Come close to me!" And Julian, lifting the cloth, lay down on the dead leaves side by side with him. The leper turned his head. "Take off thy clothes, that I may have thy body's warmth!" Julian took off his clothes and lay down on the bed again, naked as when he was born; and he felt the leper's skin against his thigh, colder than a serpent and rough as a file. He tried to hearten him, and the other answered in grasps: "Ah, I am dying! Come closer, warm me! Not with hands; no, with thy body!"
>
> Julian stretched himself completely over him, mouth to mouth, and chest to chest. Then the leper clasped him, and his eyes suddenly became bright as stars; his hair drew out like sunbeams; the breath of his nostrils was as sweet as roses; a cloud of incense rose from the hearth, and the waves began to sing. Meanwhile, an abundance of delight, a superhuman joy flooded Julian's soul as he lay swooning; and he who still clasped him in his arms grew taller, ever taller, until his head and feet touched the two walls of the hut. The roof flew off, the

firmament unrolled—and Julian rose towards the blue spaces, face to face with our Lord Jesus, who carried him to heaven.[61]

Dorothy Day was an American saint, her devotion to the poor and needy comparable to Mother Teresa's. But, unlike Mother Teresa, Day repeatedly confessed her limitations, her fatigue with the ceaseless daily chores, her all-too-human revulsion for contact with the great unwashed. "Sometimes, as in St. Francis's case, freedom from fastidiousness, and detachment from worldly things, can be obtained in only one step. We would like to think this is often so. And yet the older I get the more I see that life is made up of many steps, and they are very small ones, not giant strides. I have 'kissed a leper' not once but twice—consciously—yet I cannot say I am much the better for it. The second time I was refusing a bed to a drunken prostitute with a huge, toothless, rouged mouth, a nightmare of a mouth. . . . I had to deny this woman a bed, and when she asked me to kiss her I did, and it was a loathsome thing, the way she did it."[62]

Courage and Heroism

I have often wondered how I would behave if I were in danger and whether I would act bravely in situations that require bravery. For this reason, I was struck by the following incident reported in the *Minneapolis Tribune* soon after my arrival in Minneapolis. It occurred on Hennepin Avenue, which was close to where I lived. "I was with my wife and this guy came on us with a gun. He held it on her and that frightened me, but I didn't do anything, I couldn't. But somehow I kept calm. Then he put the gun on my head and before I knew it I was on my hands and knees crying and pleading. I cried about how my kids needed me and how I gave him everything we had and I just fell apart, I fell absolutely apart."[63]

Two boys acted heroically under very different circumstances. The first is Malcolm Muggeridge. The headmaster of his school, a man named Hillyer, was known to have a sadistic love of caning boys. "These caning occasions . . . became routine events for many of the boys. In order to prevent the boys from putting exercise books in their trousers to soften the blows, Hillyer would have them lower their trousers to the ground. One day when a caning session was in progress in the library, Malcolm walked in, grabbed the cane out of Hillyer's hands, broke it, and walked out without uttering a word. Nothing was ever said about the incident, but it made him, for a time, the school hero."[64]

The second example of young courage is reported by Simone Weil. She participated briefly in the Spanish Civil War, during which she witnessed the following incident. "In a light engagement a small party of militiamen from various countries captured a boy of fifteen who was a member of the Falange. As soon as he was captured, and still trembling from the sight of his comrades being killed alongside him, he said he had been enrolled compulsorily. He was searched and a medal of the Virgin and a Falange card was found on him. Then he was sent to Durruti, the leader of the column, who lectured him for an hour on the beauties of the anarchist ideal and gave him the choice between death and enrolling immediately in the ranks of his captors, against his comrades of yesterday. Durruti gave this child twenty-four hours to think it over, and when the time was up he said no and was shot."[65]

George Orwell, who also participated in the Spanish Civil War, presented yet another image of someone young, good, and brave. An Italian volunteer whom he had met for only a moment in a barracks in Barcelona "was standing in profile to me, his chin on his breast, gazing with a puzzled frown at a map which one of the officers had upon the table. Something in his face deeply moved me. It was the face of a man who would commit murder and throw away his life for a friend. There were both candor and ferocity in it; also the pathetic reverence that illiterate people have for their supposed superiors. Obviously he could not make head or tail of the map; obviously he regarded map-reading as a stupendous intellectual feat." Several years afterward, Orwell wrote that, although he never saw the man again, the impression of selfless courage was his most vivid memory of the entire war.[66]

On the night of 10 October 1975 eighteen-year-old Bradley VanDamme was involved in a serious one-car accident. "As he lay unconscious in the front seat, the rear of his vehicle burst into flames. By the time bystander Billie Joe McCullough reached the car, the fire had spread into the front passenger compartment. McCullough crawled into the car and, with great difficulty and at obvious risk to his own life, pulled VanDamme free. Moments later the entire car exploded into flames. Although VanDamme suffered extensive injuries and was badly burnt, he eventually recovered." McCullough, a twenty-two-year-old laborer, was later awarded the Carnegie Medal, an honor given for "outstanding acts of selfless heroism performed in the United States and Canada."[67]

One cold evening, a man is crossing a bridge and hears a splash. Someone has fallen into the canal. The man who hears the splash can swim, but he does not attempt a rescue. Instead, he debates the pros and cons of taking action until it is too late to do anything. This story from Albert Camus' novel *The Fall* made me uncomfortable when I first read it in 1957. "I am that man," I couldn't help thinking. The man I would like to be—and can only be in my daydreams—is Lenny Skutnick.

On 13 January 1982 an Air Florida plane crashed into the icy Potomac River. Skutnick dived into it. At great risk to himself, he saved a woman's life. The hero himself had to be taken to the hospital, for his body temperature had dropped dangerously low in the rescue attempt. When he eventually went home, he was bombarded by questions from neighbors and reporters. Why did he

do it? How was he able to muster the courage to jump in? Skutnick seemed puzzled. He said: "She was going under. I was right
there watching. She was going to drown if no one moved. I
jumped in."[68]

Both McCullough and Skutnick responded heroically to the
demand of the moment. They were civilians, by which I mean
that it was not their job to save victims of car and airplane acci-
dents. Policemen and firemen, by contrast, are in professions that
require them to put themselves in positions of danger. They are
psychologically primed for bravery. When they act bravely in the
line of duty, they are nevertheless greatly and rightly admired, for
no matter how rigorous the training, self-sacrifice goes against the
grain of human nature.

Guy Willoughby is in a category by himself. He wasn't responding to the urgent needs of the moment, as McCullough and
Skutnick were. He also wasn't doing something courageous in the
clear line of duty, as does a fireman, policeman, or soldier. Here is
the story as reported in the *New York Times* on 3 December 1989.
One day in November 1989, Guy Willoughby "shed the natty suit
that he has frequently worn in Kabul, dropped to his hands and
knees off a highway north of here, and worked his way through
a Soviet mine field. Using a metal detector, a probe and his
hands, Mr. Willoughby, a former Guards officer in the British
Army, lifted enough mines to clear a narrow path. That done, the

twenty-nine-year-old Englishman and a companion, Paul Jefferson, cleared another, smaller minefield nearby. Back in Kabul, Mr. Willoughby, a great-grandson of a former viceroy of India, departed for a vacation in England, where his passions included horse breeding and polo." Noblesse oblige hasn't totally disappeared in our time.

Moral Courage

Moral courage is as life threatening as physical courage, for it isolates individuals from their fellow humans, on whose support their well-being and, ultimately, life depend. As with physical courage, moral courage—at least in its extreme form—seems a gift: one either has it or one doesn't. No doubt it can be inculcated, but inculcation (i.e., education) can only go so far. Albert Schweitzer showed moral courage when he made himself subject to ridicule in his ardent promotion of a "reverence for life." Why argue for compassion for all living things, even the mosquito, when he could rest his laurels on such unambiguous achievements as his musical and theological scholarship and his effort to relieve pain among Africans in Africa?

Malcolm Muggeridge, as a boy, had the physical courage to snatch the cane from a sadistic schoolmaster, break it in two, and walk out. As a man he consistently showed not only physical but also moral courage by telling the truth as he saw it, even if this meant the ostracism of his peers and the loss of his job, as happened more than once. Since I am an academic who constantly feels pressure from activist students to support their cause, however poorly thought through, I am particularly impressed by Muggeridge's ability to withstand such pressure, which was at its height in the 1960s.

In 1966 Muggeridge was elected rector of Edinburgh University by the Student Representative Council, no doubt for his reputation as a maverick and an outspoken critic of the British establishment. The job of rector was largely ceremonial; its one designated nonceremonial obligation was to pass students' wishes and concerns on to the university's governing body. Well, in 1967 the students wanted to have free pot and birth-control pills on campus. Muggeridge received their request, but, instead of dealing with it through the usual channels, he gave his response in his Annual Rectorial Address on 14 January 1968. Normally, rectors used this great public occasion to play to the gallery, especially to the students' gallery, for rectors were, after all, elected by students. This time, the new rector spoke like an outraged Old Testament prophet. He said that he would have understanding for almost any act of insubordination against the rundown, spiritually impoverished society that was Britain. But, rather than direct his righteous anger against it, he directed it toward the students: "How infinitely sad; how, in a macabre sort of way, funny, that the form . . . [student] insubordination takes should be a demand for pot and pills, for the most tenth-rate sort of escapism and self-indulgence ever known! . . . The resort of any old, slobbering debauchee anywhere in the world at any time—dope and bed."[69]

Would I, decked in rectorial or professorial robe, dare to face the shock of disappointment and disapproval—the sullen silence, the hisses and boos—when instead, by offering the usual pablum of uplifting rhetoric, I can fill my ears with waves of applause? I suspect not.

Political courage is moral courage—the carrying through of a moral principle even if it goes against popular sentiment, even if it brings about personal calumny and damages the political fortune of one's party, and even if some awful consequences are likely to follow. In the United States, Lincoln is without question the outstanding exemplar of such courage. He risked the calamity of civil war so that slavery, that ultimate injustice, might be abolished. A more ambiguous example of moral political courage was Charles de Gaulle's decision to grant independence to Algeria in 1961. He did so against his own vision of a Greater France that stretched from Calais at La Manche (the English Channel) to Tamanrasset in the Sahara. He did so because he had the lucidity to see the inevitable secession of Algeria from France; but, apart from this political realism, he also had the rectitude to recognize the right of a people, only recently linked to the "mother" country, to choose their own destiny. He took the step toward Algerian independence even though he knew that violence would erupt, that freed Algeria would hardly show him gratitude, that he would be hated by a significant number of his countrymen on both sides of the Mediterranean Sea, and that assassins would tail him for the rest of his life.[70]

Courage exercised by people of power like Lincoln and de Gaulle has consequences for many people. Courage exercised by an individual of little power has no such consequences—not, at least, in the short run. Only his or her own fate will be affected. Nonetheless, he or she is a hero. First Lt. Ehren K. Watada of the United States Army is such a hero. He was a promising young officer rated among the best by his superiors. Like many young men after 11 September 2001 he volunteered out of a desire to protect his country. Intellectually curious, he started to read about the war in Iraq, beginning with James Bamford's book *A Pretext for War,* which argues that neoconservative civilians in the Pentagon twisted intelligence to justify the toppling of Saddam Hussein. Watada went on to other publications on related war themes, including selections on the treatment of prisoners at Guantánamo Bay. He also started to talk with soldiers returning from Iraq. Shocked and disgusted, he delivered a passionate two-page letter to his brigade commander, Col. Stephen Townsend, on 25 January 2006, asking to resign his commission. Watada insisted that he was not a conscientious objector. He was willing to fight and requested that he be transferred to Afghanistan, where—he believed—military operations were far better justified. But his request was rejected. A soldier could not pick and choose where to do battle. Watada understood that. Nevertheless, in his letter to Colonel Townsend he said that, in the case of Iraq, he owed allegiance to a "higher power"—the Constitution—based on the values the army had taught him: "loyalty, duty, respect, selfless service, honor, integrity, and personal courage." Watada embodied these values when he served in South Korea. Recommendations from his peers and superiors were glowing. Watada has the makings of a great soldier and patriot. He must have known that this one act of conscience meant not only the prospect of court-martial, the end of his military career, but also social ostracism and incomprehension on the part of his family and friends.[71]

2

Doing Good in the Midst of Evil

The vignettes of virtue I have provided so far are taken mostly from "normal" life, by which I mean life in a functioning civil society not actively engaged in war. Moreover, except in the examples of physical attractiveness and good manners, they are mostly *single* instances of virtue occurring under the demands of particular occasions. Thus, Lenny Skutnick sees a woman drowning and jumps into icy water to save her; thereafter, he returns to normal life. Guy Willoughby crawls in the fields of Afghanistan to defuse mines left there during the Afghan-Soviet War; having done as much as he can, he returns to the England of afternoon tea and polo. What if these people lived not in normal society but in one stained by the evil of fascism? How would they behave? Is there a personality difference between those able to confront the single life-threatening challenge with outstanding courage and those whose courage is tested by the possibility of imprisonment, if not immediate death, day after day, even year after year?

Doing good in the midst of evil—that's the story of the rescuers of Jews in Nazi-occupied Europe. The rescuers were a small minority. Why they did what most of their countrymen were unwilling or afraid to do remains largely a mystery. We do know, however, that the rescuers were an extraordinary mix of rich and poor, highly educated and barely literate—peasants, urban workers, landowners, businessmen, aristocrats, the religious, and those who professed no particular faith. Christians among the rescuers almost always quoted the passage about the Good Samaritan as a source of inspiration: one must always come to the help of one's neighbor—and the neighbor can be anybody. But nonbelievers were also committed to helping the stranger in need because in their eyes no one was a stranger—the person they helped was in a deep sense the same as them. Why these Europeans saw the world that way surely owed something to their Christian heritage, even if the source went unacknowledged or was denied.

Other commonalities among the rescuers include the denial that they were heroes or even that they did anything out of the ordinary. Their conviction of the rightness of what they did was so strong that they could barely imagine people who could act otherwise and not know that they had betrayed the core of their being. Most rescuers were nonpolitical in the sense that they did not see themselves as acting out of patriotism, internationalism, an abstract ideal of the "brotherhood of mankind," or saving a people called the Jews. When the Vichy police came for the Jews hiding in Le Chambon, the villagers faux-innocently asked, "Jews? We don't know any Jews." They could proclaim ignorance without feeling that they had told a blatant lie because they recognized only individuals; they identified with and had compassion for a particular man, a particular woman, a particular child, each with a distinctive name and personality, rather than with a whole group or race.

The rescuers did not expect to be thanked. Remarkably, they sometimes felt that they were the ones to give thanks. For what? For being afforded an opportunity to be of service to their fellow humans. We can better understand this attitude if we remember that the rescuers did not suffer the anguish of indecision. They never debated what they should and should not do, totaling up the cost of action and inaction, for they never felt they had any choice. Their moral freedom—their sense of exhilaration—lay, paradoxically, in not having freedom. How "anguish of choice" differs from "joy of obedience" is strikingly illustrated in the following incident.

A Dutch pastor came into the watch repair shop of the Ten Booms. Corrie ten Boom, the daughter of the house and an active rescuer, took the pastor aside and asked him whether he would take a Jewish mother and baby into his home, the safest place for them. Corrie brought the baby down for the pastor to see with his own eyes. She wrote: "Back in the dining room I pulled back

the coverlet from the baby's face. There was a long silence. The
man bent forward. . . . For a moment I saw compassion and fear
struggle in his face. Then he straightened. 'No. Definitely not. We
could lose our lives for that Jewish child!' Unseen by either of us,
Father had appeared in the doorway. 'Give the child to me, Corrie,' he said. Father held the baby close, his white beard brushing
its cheek, looking into the little face. . . . At last he looked up at
the pastor, 'You say we could lose our lives for this child. I would
consider that the greatest honor that could come to my family.'"[1]

I am awestruck by what Corrie's father said. The utterance and
the commitment that went with it is our birthright as the children
of God. How sad that most of us would have acted like the pastor
rather than Corrie's father. Yet the pastor was a moral man. He
made a moral choice that just happened to favor himself and
those closest to him. "Many thoroughly decent [Christian] people
chose not to rescue, not because of a lack of courage but due to
the moral conviction that their obligations to their own families
and neighbors were primary. They believed that to risk their loved
ones' and their neighbors' lives on behalf of strangers would be
morally irresponsible."[2]

The Trocmés of Le Chambon

Doing good in the midst of evil is the glory of Le Chambon, a
village in southern France. In the course of four years of German

occupation, three thousand impoverished Chambonnais villagers saved the lives of five thousand Jewish refugees. They were able to do so in large part because of the inspired leadership of Pastor André Trocmé and his wife, Magda. These two—André and Magda—were a living demonstration of how good people could have very different temperaments, do good in very different ways, yet become one at those critical points when another human being is in danger.

André was a passionately religious man, creative and touched by mysticism. The mystic strain was so strong that, as a student at the Union Theological Seminary in New York, he found the Social Gospel movement prevalent in the 1920s too rational, too worldly. It was only after marrying Magda that he learned to see the righteousness and religious significance of devotion to neighbor—the second of the two greatest commandments. André's passionate nature was not by any means confined to his theological beliefs. His warmth toward people had an almost erotic charge to it. A friend said, "He wanted to hug you—yes, even to kiss you." A refugee enthused over his smile, "That smile . . . that smile!" Another refugee compared his presence to a rousing performance of Beethoven's "Eroica" Symphony that impelled one to rise to the highest level of generosity and joy. André's giving nature warmed others and made them also want to be giving: he made "good" infectious, a threat to the world of evil and indifference.

And then there was his creativity—his knack for finding new ways to do things, new ways to hide refugees from the Vichy police, new ways to subvert persecuting officialdom, new ways to make the most of extremely limited resources and create a social atmosphere that minimized conflict in crowded conditions. "Good" could seem vapid or conformist. Moralists have argued against conformity to society's deadening rules in favor of heeding the buried, erotically charged impulses of life. André looked under the surface of society and its rules of behavior, but what he found underneath was not volcanic *eros;* rather, it was *caritas,* Jesus's call for new ways of seeing and acting toward one's fellow human beings or, in less specifically Christian terms, a seed of supernal goodness that awaited fruition.

Compared with André, Magda was less formally religious. Raised as a Catholic and placed for a time in a convent, she rebelled against the academism and strictures of religion, professing to André at the time of their courtship that she was neither Catholic nor Protestant but that religious life, for her, was loving one's neighbor as oneself in the details of caring. She gave physical comfort to people. Philip Hallie put it this way: "When you cover somebody with a blanket or sweater, you are not seeking that person's spiritual salvation; you are concerned only for his or her bodily welfare. And when you cover people, you are allowing their own heat to warm their bodies under that blanket or sweater; you are not intruding on those bodies. You are only permitting them to keep well by their own body heat. In this image of covering lies the essence of Magda's way of caring for others."[3]

As to how Magda responded to refugees who came to her door, she told this story to Hallie: "A German woman knocked at my door. It was in the evening and she said she was a German Jew, coming from northern France, that she was in danger, and that she had heard that in Le Chambon somebody could help her. Could she come into my house? I said, 'Naturally, come in, come in.'" Magda settled the German woman by the stove and then went out in the bitter cold to seek out the mayor, for she saw immediately that the woman was in mortal danger unless she had identification papers. Rather naively, she expected the mayor to issue them: after all, he was a Frenchman, not a German or a Nazi. The mayor, however, said angrily, "What? Do you dare to endanger this whole village for the sake of one foreigner? Will you save one woman and destroy us all? How dare you suggest such a thing to me?" Magda did not argue with him. She realized that she had to quickly find a home for the German woman elsewhere, since the mayor—and soon everyone in the neighborhood—would know that a Jew was in her home.

A family located at some distance from Le Chambon was found for Magda's visitor to live with, and presumably she survived the occupation. But my point in telling the story here is to contrast the mayor's attitude with that of Magda. For him, there was a sharp distinction between "one of us" and "one of them," between Gentiles and Jews. The authorities had made that perfectly clear, and it was his duty as mayor to follow the rules they propagated, especially since—as he could point out—these rules were widely accepted among the French. For Magda, there was no "us" and "them." When someone knocked on her door, seeking refuge, the answer could only be "Naturally, come in, come in." And, of course, this was also exactly André's position.[4]

What were the costs to the Trocmés and the villagers of Le Chambon when they protected Jewish refugees first from Vichy policemen and later from SS soldiers? If they had been caught, the penalty would almost certainly have been deportation and, with it, the loss of property and, very likely, of life. Every day, during the four years of occupation, the villagers and especially their leaders, the Trocmés, lived under this threat. Their courage was under constant call, and they could never know when the ultimate sacrifice would be required of them. Meanwhile, stress steadily built up as, week after week, more and more refugees poured in. At one time, some sixty refugees were hidden in the presbytery alone. Just because the Jews were victims did not mean that they were saints or even likable. A girl from a wealthy family demanded breakfast in bed, one young man insisted that his girlfriend be allowed to visit him, and another refused to eat anything that wasn't kosher.

These irritations were added to the ones the hosts might expect to shoulder, such as giving up space, food, and the little comforts and conveniences they were used to. Hardest of all for the adults of Le Chambon was to require their own children to eat less so that the food they had could be more widely shared.[5]

That the Chambonnais survived the occupation was a testament to their extraordinary resourcefulness and adaptability. Both were supported by a love for their fellow human beings that was the opposite of willed charity. Prolonged over time, willed charity might easily degenerate into resentment. No doubt there was some resentment among the rescuers: that would only be human. But not much, for the rescuers claimed to have found satisfaction using their minds and hearts to help people in need. When interviewers pressed Magda once too often on her extraordinary sense of responsibility, she pretended that her virtue was just an attempt to obtain pleasure: "I get pleasure from doing such things—yes, pleasure, the way some people get pleasure from the movies. It amuses me to help somebody, no matter what the cost."[6]

The villagers of Le Chambon coped with external threats—Vichy policemen and SS soldiers who were obliged to arrest villagers if they found Jews in their homes—by cunningly using verbal and gestural subterfuges. Repeatedly, they managed to disobey the law without appearing to do so. This way, they left intact the dignity and amour propre of the officers of the law and so disinclined them from ruthless persecution. In other words, the Trocmés and, following their example, the villagers did not categorize whole groups of people as the enemy and so were better able to avoid direct confrontation. When an individual Vichy policeman or SS soldier came to the presbytery to do his unsavory job, he was treated courteously and might even be offered dinner if it was already on the table.

Good, Evil, and Stupidity

The villagers of Le Chambon were good people, inspired by the Trocmés to be heroically good. Their virtue was such that it diffused beyond Le Chambon to farms and villages throughout south-central France, creating (as it were) "points of light" in a land darkened by prejudice and fear. Would we say that evil had befallen this land? Certainly, the degree of evil to be found there did not match that which swamped the much smaller concentration camps. Even in a concentration camp, points of light might flicker, but they were powerless to spread and had the effect of making the surrounding darkness seem even darker. South-central France under the Vichy government was not so much evil as blighted, morally obtuse. What Pastor André Trocmé discovered when he sought help for refugees in places outside Le Chambon was, to the pastor's surprise, righteous indignation. French men and women, and especially the law officers among them, were genuinely shocked that the pastor, himself a figure of law, could ask them to hide Jews, an act that was declared illegal. And more than that, they thought the request unpatriotic, for they readily accepted the semiofficial line that Jews were the cause of French decadence and the downfall of their country. Did the people accept government propaganda from the need to feel safe on the side of power, or did they do so out of deep-seated prejudice, a real distaste for all who differed from them, a prejudice that could be exploited for a far larger evil purpose?

We can never know. André's conclusion was that human beings fall under more than the two categories of good and evil and that there was a third—stupidity. Over and over again, stupidity rather than outright evil proves to be society's downfall. Can a good person be stupid? Can a stupid person be good? But then, what is "stupidity," and what, for that matter, is "good"? "Stupidity" seems to be a willful narrowing and dimming of one's vision caused by anxiety and the fear of an ego that ceaselessly requires protection and fattening. "Good" is the opposite. I need to develop these points, and I will do so in the last section of the book. But, first, let me expand the overall data for thinking about human goodness by looking into the life stories of six individuals.

3

Good Individuals

Their Life Stories

One feels instinctively that goodness cannot be just one act, that it has to be an overall quality, almost innate, like a characteristic smile or tone of voice that is sustained over a lifetime. But, if so, does this mean that the thief on the cross was not a good man even though, after showing signs of contrition, Christ forgave him and said that he would enter Paradise? And was even Saint Paul good? As Saul he was a persecuting bigot, but on the road to Damascus he heard Christ's voice and converted: he became Paul, a good man, a saint.

A major change from bad to good, if it occurs, does so through God's grace—that is to say, miraculously, as the two examples I have given illustrate. Gradual change, by contrast, can be effected by education. Even then, I am inclined to think that what was deemed "bad" wasn't really bad in the first place but rather was a quality that could be channeled, with proper encouragement and nurturing, to become a virtue, as, for example, rashness into courage, hesitancy into prudence, and indiscriminate spending into generosity. There is also the difference between an ordinary act and one that is, by all measures, exceptional. Simple good manners fall under what I call "ordinary acts." They contribute to the quality of life, as I pointed out earlier. But it may well happen that someone with exquisite manners on the public stage is evil in private life. Also, small gestures of helpfulness, occasionally rendered, do not reveal the whole person. But when the act is exceptional—Jane Smith's offer of her kidney to a sick student, for instance—I believe that it is truly revelatory. She is, we say, like that.

Of the six good persons I introduce in the following section, two—Confucius and Socrates—are from antiquity. We know very little about their childhood and youth and so cannot know whether they turned from bad to good. All the available evidence indicates, however, that no such shift occurred and that, in fact, all six persons showed remarkable consistency: they were good from the beginning and remained good, their life course being more in the nature of a rosebud turning into a rose than an acorn turning into a tree.

Confucius (ca. 551–479 BCE)

Confucius lost his father at age three and grew up under strait-
ened circumstances under his mother's care. As a boy he liked to set
up sacrificial vessels and imitate the gestures of ritual. He married
at age nineteen. He and his wife produced a son and two daugh-
ters. The marriage was far from ideal. Confucius, who placed family at the center of his worldview, ironically did not himself enjoy a
happy family life. While still a young man he entered the service of
a noble family as superintendent of parks and herds. At thirty-two
he found employment teaching ancient rituals to a minister's sons.
At thirty-three he went to Lo-yang, the imperial capital, to study
the customs and traditions of the Chou royal house. After Confucius had been in the capital for one year the prince of Lu—
Confucius's patron—was forced to flee. Confucius accompanied
him and, while in exile, deepened his scholarship and learned to
appreciate music. At age fifty-one he became a minister in the state
of Lu. The state flourished, but unfortunately the prince was cor-
rupted by dancing girls and fine horses and neglected government
affairs. Confucius quit his job. He traveled far and wide in the
hope that his prince would call him back or that some other prince
would seek his counsel. No such call came. At age sixty-eight he returned to his native state of Lu and busied himself with studying
the *I Ching* and with teaching a group of young men.

This is Confucius's life story in a nutshell. Significant is the fact that even as a boy he was interested in ritual, that as a young man he taught ancient customs and traditions to a minister's sons, and that he felt the need to go to Lo-yang for further study. He could have made himself a brilliant career as scholar and teacher, but he wanted more, which was to serve the people in government. Confucius never managed to attain high office, but some of his students did. One might wonder why the rulers of his time would want to hire them, since they were taught the proprieties of the ancient classics and not practical administration. An answer might be that, however unruly and unscrupulous the rulers were themselves, they knew their states would collapse without honest and disciplined administrators and without men familiar with the ancient rituals that were the grounds of civility. Confucius was well equipped to provide these talents.

Significant also about Confucius is that although as a young man he supervised parks and herds for a noble family, nature—in sharp contrast to Lao-tzu—was never for him a source of inspiration or solace. To Confucius and Confucians, "natural" came close to mean "raw." Confucius conjured an image of ancient times when "in winter, the rulers lived in caves which they had excavated, and in summer in nests which they had framed. They knew not yet the transforming power of fire, but ate the fruits of plants and trees and the flesh of birds and beasts. . . . They knew not yet the use of flax and silk, but clothed themselves with feathers and skins."[1] This being so, it followed that we owe our civilized state to the invention and knowledge of our forebears, who, therefore, were to be revered, their knowledge and accomplishments maintained and improved upon. As for nature, it was to be respected but not valued so highly that it exacted a cost in human welfare. It was said of Confucius that "he angled, but did not use a net; he shot, but not at sitting birds."[2] When his stable burned down, Confucius, returning from court, asked, "Was anyone hurt? He did not ask about the horses" (*Analects* 10:12). While this showed an admirable concern for human life, it also showed an indifference to the fate of the horses. Confucius clinched his bias in favor not only of human life but of human culture in his response to a student who questioned the killing of a sheep as an element in a sacrificial rite. "You love sheep, I love ceremony" was Confucius's reply (*Analects* 3:17).

In social matters, Confucius's stature needs to be seen in the context of his time, which was one in which kings and princes strove ruthlessly for power and prestige. True, they also made an effort to maintain the ancient rituals and ceremonies, but they did so largely because they saw them as serving the purpose of enhancing their status and power. The performances, for this reason, tended to become more and more showy. Confucius said irritably, "Eight rows of dancers danced in his court. If this could be tolerated, what could not be tolerated?" (*Analects* 3:1). And "surely when the ancients said 'ritual,' they did not have in mind only jade and silk. And surely when they said 'music,' they did not merely refer to bells and drums" (*Analects* 17:10). Needless to say, Confucius's attempts at correcting the public and private excesses of the rulers met with little success.

The rulers were annoyed by Confucius's tireless urging, but when it was directed only at ritual and personal conduct it did not seriously threaten their power. What did threaten their power and would have radically altered society was Confucius's idea that hereditary kingship should yield to the rule of the wise. Knowing that such a radical idea could not possibly be realized and that advocacy of it could well cost him his head, he urged, more practically, the kings to hire only good and wise ministers; for Confucius, the prime test of "good" was a genuine concern for the welfare of the people, and a test of "wise" was the ability to govern by example and persuasion rather than by setting up rigid laws and the use of force.

Confucius seems to have truly sympathized with plain folks, a sympathy that might have had its origin in his own childhood, which was lived in genteel poverty, and in the fact that he got to know and came to like peasants and laborers in his first job as superintendent of parks and herds. His heart was in the right place. As for his ability to govern, during the one time Confucius enjoyed executive power, he used it well. This was in 501 BCE, when Confucius was appointed chief magistrate of Zhong-du in his home state of Lu. Zhong-du was so well governed that it served as a model for other towns and cities in the region. "It was said that an article dropped in the streets would not be stolen, but would instead be found by its owner exactly where he left it. . . . Funeral customs were streamlined, and ostentatious burials became a thing of the past."[3]

Confucius, though wise in his dealings with subordinates, was not so wise—or, rather, not so worldly-wise—in his dealings with his superiors. This was one reason why, other than the position of chief magistrate, he had only honorific roles and sinecures. The powerful welcomed Confucius in their midst for prestige—after all, everyone agreed that he was an exceptionally learned man—and as a token of their own virtue. When Confucius, dissatisfied with the absence of serious employment, wanted to leave, his patrons made only a show of persuading him to stay. They were at a loss as to what to do with a man whose virtue was such that he disdained intrigue and was constitutionally unable to flatter, a man who eschewed even eloquence, which he compared to the superfluous embroideries he found and disliked in the rituals and ceremonies of his time. The fact that at least some of Confucius's students occupied high office would suggest that they did not learn bluntness from their teacher.

Confucius had revolutionary ideas that he obtained, like many other revolutionaries in the world, by looking back to an idealized past. What the past gave him was an image of human relationship as holy dance, analogous to the cosmic dance that one could see in heaven. "Holy dance" implies a certain stateliness, and stateliness can degenerate into dry formality. Confucius, aware of this danger, insisted that stateliness be enlivened by genuine feeling, as it did (he assumed) in the time of the original founders and virtuous kings. Two key words in the thought of Confucius and his followers were *jen* and *li;* together they made the dance possible and ensured that it would be genuinely felt. *Jen* is the natural affection of people for one another. It is exhibited in all kinds of human relations but outstandingly in those between parents and children, old and young. *Li* originally meant "sacrifice" or "sacrificial ritual"—words that had an ominous undertone, for they referred back to a distant past when human beings had to appease supernatural powers with animal and even human sacrifice. Either Confucius did not know this ominous meaning or he chose to ignore it. Instead, he humanized *li* so that it covered only human behavior, but within human behavior it was inclusive: court rites and diplomatic relations were *li,* but so were the most frequent and ordinary encounters in the home and on the street.

Jen and *li,* practiced together, meant that in every human exchange there was a degree of solemnity, a degree of respect, and a degree of feeling or affection. Everyone had to be treated courteously if only because everyone—whatever his or her social status—was part of a dance, beautiful and harmonious, as music could be beautiful and harmonious. To Confucius, music was not something added on as a decoration to rites and ceremonies but was, rather, the embodiment in sound of their very spirit and essence. In a deep sense, even the smallest gesture, such as greeting a friend, should evoke music's sweet harmony.[4]

Confucius lived in a world that couldn't be further removed from this idyllic picture. The rulers of his time paid only lip service to *li* and *jen*. Religion declined into superstition, morality into "might is right" and calculations of expediency and convenience. Human life was extremely cheap. "Duke Ling of the great state of Chin enjoyed shooting at the passers-by from a tower, to watch them try to dodge his missiles; when his cook did not prepare bears' paws to his taste he had the cook killed." Punishments were not only cruel but frequent. "In the state of Ch'i, mutilation of the feet was so usual that special footgear was sold in the shops for those who had suffered it."[5] Officials used bribery to benefit themselves and their relatives and might even hire assassins to get rid of a rival.

How, under these circumstances, should the good man live? What would he be like? What are his characteristics? Without doubt, the picture of the good man Confucius formulated was one he himself hoped to be, and so to know it is also to know something of Confucius the man.

Confucius considered the sage, someone born with insight to truth and goodness, to be the highest category of the good man and gave Yao, Shun, and Yu, the original founders of society, as examples. Sages, however, are the rare exception, as are also people who are too stupid to learn or who simply make no effort. Most people lie somewhere in the middle. A good man is one who strives to learn and persists until he succeeds. He pushes himself and is pulled by the nobility of the goal. He has a genial temperament, is independent, and strives to be just. He copes equally well with misfortune and prosperity. He is free from fear, and if he suffers it is from awareness of his own defects rather than from external circumstances. He seeks to match his words with action so that words don't become just empty sounds. He is dedicated and disciplined yet is not competitive, except in leisure-time activities such as archery (*Analects* 3:7).

Confucius never considered himself a sage, but he did strive to know all that could be known. A man of his time, he took the existence of spirits and omens for granted. Certainly, ancestor cult was central to his belief and practice, yet he showed his critical temperament and rationality by deliberately avoiding the topic of magical powers and by confining the cult of spirits to the cult of ancestors. "If you cannot serve men, how can you serve spirits? If you do not understand life, how can you understand death?" were the sort of remark that indicated his agnosticism (*Analects* 11:12). Confucius often spoke of heaven (*tien*), but only once of lord (*shang-ti*). Heaven, in other words, was impersonal. It showered wealth and prestige and it destroyed, impersonally. Confucius seldom mentioned prayer, and when he did it was not petitionary and certainly not magical. Heaven was a source of inspiration rather than of power. "Only heaven is great. The seasons go their course and all things come into being. But does heaven speak?" (*Analects* 17:18).

By posing the question, Does heaven speak? Confucius implied that order in heaven was achieved without striving, without even the help of speech, which was seen as a form of action. Ideally, human society should also be able to maintain order with an air of effortlessness (*Analects* 2:1). For this to happen, however, one must begin not with society but with the self—with self-cultivation, self-perfection—and then, more by example than by action, persuade others to do the same. Confucius referred to the legendary emperor Shun, "who achieved good government by merely sitting with dignity, facing south. That is all" (*Analects* 15: 5). In speaking thus, Confucius revealed a streak of Taoism in him. But, predominantly, he was an activist. He favored action and he did speak. He spoke "truth to power."

Power, however, did not take kindly to truth. The one high position Confucius had, a seat on the Council of State, he soon found to be largely a sinecure. Rather than accept a life of ineffectual ease, Confucius boldly set off in search of another ruler who would listen to him. He wandered over the face of China, a learned yet unsophisticated man who encountered hardships on the road and courteous but insincere treatment from princes in the cities. There was a touch of the ridiculous in the travels of a man of nearly sixty years—quite old for someone of his time—still driven by his ideals, but, as H. G. Creel put it, it was a "magnificent kind of ridiculousness, found only in the great."[6]

Confucius began teaching at age twenty-three and then again more or less full time at age fifty-five, when he was looking unsuccessfully for a ministerial position. Though frustrated in government service, in teaching Confucius found fulfillment and success. Early on, his students were friends who were not much younger than he, so it would be more accurate to speak of their meetings as like those of a debating society in which members could speak more or less as equals. From the start, then, the Confucian teaching style had a degree of openness and informality that was quite the exception in China at that time and in China even now. (The difference from India's guru-disciple model couldn't be more striking.) Of course, when Confucius reached his midfifties and some of his students were teenagers, a more asymmetrical relationship developed. Nevertheless, Confucius continued to encourage questioning, but, even more, he demanded hard work, seriousness, and a modicum of talent. "If I present one corner of a subject, and my students cannot deduce the other three, I do not repeat my lesson" (*Analects* 7:8).

Confucius accepted students from all backgrounds, regardless of wealth or social status. "If someone were willing to bring me a bundle of dried meat in payment, I would still not refuse to instruct him" (*Analects* 7:7). He even took in a man who had served a term in prison; this man in time became one of his best students, and Confucius liked him well enough to give his daughter to him in marriage (*Analects* 5:1). Some of the students thought it only natural that Confucius's son received special instruction from his father. This was not the case, nor did Confucius favor the sons of privilege in any way. One great appeal of Confucius as a teacher was that he respected the young. "A young person," he said, "should be treated with the utmost respect. How do you know that he will not, one day, be fully the equal of what you are now? It is the man who has reached the age of forty or fifty without having done anything to distinguish himself who is not worthy of respect" (*Analects* 9:22).

What else can we say of Confucius? He was devoted to music, lauded it as a source of pleasure, played the lute, and took part in informal group singing. But music meant far more to him than just a pastime or a social mucilage. He believed that it could teach one how to act properly in society and could even affect the way one unconsciously moved. In his journeys he could tell when he had entered a civilized area by observing the way peasants worked in the fields, the way villagers dealt with their daily chores, and how they walked. To the driver of his carriage he commented that a boy carrying a pitcher seemed to have internalized many of the teachings of the sages' music.[7]

Confucius was self-confident yet modest. Unlike such noted teachers as Mo-tzu and Hsün-tzu, he was quick to admit his own ignorance. "To make a mistake and not correct it is a mistake indeed" (*Analects* 15:30). Modesty also showed in his conversations, which frequently revealed a sense of humor that gave bad moments to pious commentators of a later age. He disliked all pretension. Once, when he was sick and his students believed that he was at the gate of death, they dressed themselves up as though they were ministers in attendance upon a high dignitary. Confucius asked: "By making this pretense of having ministers when I have none, whom do you think I am going to deceive? Is it not better that I should die in the hands of you, my friends, than in the hands of ministers?" (*Analects* 9:11).[8]

Confucius's self-control could make him seem rather distant, a man who could not feel deeply about another. But this was not so.

In old age Confucius gained a new teenage protégé by the name of Yan Hui who was shy and quiet. Confucius said jokingly of him, "Yan Hui is no help to me, because he agrees with everything I say. . . . He just nods like an idiot" (*Analects* 11:4, 2:9). But when Yan Hui died—and he died young—Confucius took it hard. The other students said, "You are grieving excessively, to which Confucius replied, Am I indeed? And if I am not to mourn excessively for this man, for whom am I to do so?" (*Analects* 11:9–10).

Although Confucius wanted to serve in court, he could see virtue in a life of simple pleasures. Late in life he chatted with four students, three of whom expressed a strong desire to serve the state. Confucius turned to the fourth student, Zeng Xi, who happened to be playing the zither at the time. "I am not so ambitious," said Zeng Xi. "No matter," said Confucius, "I still wish to hear your thoughts." "Well, then," said Zeng Xi, "I'd quite like a day out. My friends and I, dressed in spring finery, could take some of the boys swimming in the river, enjoy the breeze up at the Rain Altar, and come home singing." Heaving a sigh, Confucius said, "I am for Zeng Xi" (*Analects* 11:24). In moments of disillusionment Confucius spoke like a Taoist. On the other hand, he could say what no Taoist would say: "It is the man that can broaden the Way, not the Way that broadens the man" (*Analects* 15:29).

Socrates (ca. 469–399 BCE)

Surprisingly, given the cultural distance, Confucius and Socrates had much in common. Both emerged from a modest social background, contrasting, in this respect, with the Buddha. Both were physically strong. Confucius was a large man who demonstrated his vigor in old age by his arduous travels. Socrates was known for his remarkable powers of physical endurance. In his manhood he used to wear the same garment winter and summer and habitually went barefoot, even in the rigors of a winter campaign. Both Confucius and Socrates could be absentminded. Confucius, absorbed in thought, might forget to eat. Socrates' behavior was much odder. Walking with a friend, he might stop to think and stand there all night, staring into space.

Neither Confucius nor Socrates had much feeling for nature. "A man cannot live with birds and beasts. If I do not live with men, with whom shall I live?" (*Analects* 18:6). Withdrawal into nature did occur to Confucius, as we have noted, but late in life and with a sigh of regret. As for Socrates, Plato gave us a picture of him lying on a gentle grassy slope, shaded by a plane tree, engaged in dialogue. However, he supposedly said there that in his quest for knowledge he was taught by people in the city and not by fields and trees.[9] From morning to night Socrates could be found in the streets, the shops, and the gymnasiums of his beloved Athens, where he conversed with people of every age and occupation. An artisan's son, Socrates witnessed the rise of the city of Pericles under the chisels of stonemasons and sculptors. His deepest loyalty lay there.

Both Confucius and Socrates respected the farmer. Confucians, if not Confucius, eventually elevated the status of the farmer to a rank just below that of the scholar-official. Xenophon had Socrates praise agriculture as the healthiest of occupations and put into his mouth the words "the earth teaches justice too to those capable of learning."[10]

Music was central to Confucius's idea of beauty, harmony, and goodness. Socrates valued music less, perhaps to his regret, for, in prison near the end of his life, he said that he had been haunted by a dream in which he was commanded to "practice music." He did so, but to him "philosophy is the truest music."

Both Confucius and Socrates seemed somewhat ambivalent toward action—at least, toward the man of action. Of course, action could be both necessary and good. On the other hand, through ignorance or haste it could also do great harm. Confucius's golden rule was "Do *not* do to others what you would not want done to yourself." Socrates famously said that his demon always told him what *not* to do, never what to do.

Both Confucius and Socrates accepted the existence of beings—spirits, demons, gods, and goddesses—outside the human realm, but neither had the slightest interest in magic, whether black or white. Both took for granted that we owed piety to spirits and ancestors for what they had bequeathed us. Piety arose from a feeling of indebtedness. Not having a feeling of indebtedness put one at the level of the subhuman.

Although both were married and had children, neither revealed much interest in the family at a personal level. Confucius showed a theoretical interest; after all, he built his ethical system on the family. Socrates, by contrast, had no room at all for the family in his ethical system. Both men ignored half of humankind—women. Neither had a female student, though Socrates claimed that women were as educable as men. Xanthippe, Socrates' wife, was quarrelsome and physically unattractive. If she had been as beautiful as Aspasia of Miletus, the mistress of Pericles, would a woman also have been able to serve as Socrates' philosophical muse?[11] As for Confucius, it could seem unfair to accuse him of not rising above the male-centered convention of his time, but he was not just anyone, he was Confucius, a man who rose daringly above convention, when he needed to, in the political sphere.

Both Confucius and Socrates taught. There the similarity ended. Confucius *wanted* to be a teacher, especially of the rulers, so that his ideas on human relationships and government could be put into practice. Frustrated in this effort, he ended up teaching young men of lesser social standing, presumably for pay. The young men addressed him as "your excellency" in deference to his former position as a minister of justice; in time, this grand-sounding honorific (*fuzi*) meant, simply, "master" or "teacher." Socrates, by contrast, was a teacher who denied that he ever was one in the sense of possessing a body of knowledge that he wanted to pass on. He also denied that he had disciples or students. Instead, he saw himself as the unpaid head of a group of "associates" over whose studies he presided. Confucius wanted his students to be pure of heart and learned and to use those qualities to influence politics and government. Socrates, by contrast, wanted first and foremost to instill in the young an aspiration toward the Good. That some might enter government and perform honorably was fine with Socrates, but it remained a sideshow. In short, unlike Confucius, Socrates was nonpolitical, or above politics.[12]

In his relationship with his students, Confucius was correct but rather cool. On only one occasion—the death of his favorite, Yan Hui—did he show strong emotion. By contrast, Socrates was passionate. He was the lover, and the youths around him were the beloved. Socrates couldn't accept pay for his services because he could only teach—he only wanted to teach—when a boy's beauty and intelligence inspired him. As for how the boy or young man felt in Socrates' presence, this is what Alcibiades had to say: "Whenever I listen to him, my heart beats faster than if I were in a religious frenzy, and tears run down my face, and I observe that numbers of other people have had the same experience. Nothing of this kind ever used to happen to me when I listened to Pericles and other good speakers; I recognized that they spoke well, but my soul was not thrown into confusion and dismay by the thought that my life was no better than a slave's."[13]

Socrates' originality lay in granting emotion a place in thinking and education. Of the different forms that emotion could take, the one Socrates had foremost in mind was *erōs,* that is to say, sexually charged desire. *Erōs* could heat up to lust, and lust ended almost inevitably in physical assault on the object of lust. Socrates admitted to feeling sexual desire and even lust, but his self-control was such that his lower nature never had a chance to come into play. Instead, Socrates harnessed the energy in sexual desire and used it to enable him to rise to higher things. The steps of that rise were put in Socrates' mouth by Plato as follows: from passionate desire for a particular body we rise to an aesthetic enjoyment of visible beauty in general, from that to beauty of character, higher still to the intellectual beauty of the sciences, until by persevering to the end we are granted the sudden vision of Beauty itself.[14]

The path Socrates followed was one anyone could, in principle, follow. Anyone, given the desire and the discipline, could attain a vision of Beauty, which in the Greek language also meant Moral Excellence, and both were nested under the overarching concept of Good. Sublimating *erōs* to reach these higher things— these attributes of the divine—was not at all uncommon in the West. Mystics famously described the ecstasies of sexual and divine unions in identical language, thus seeming to conflate the two. As for using the one as a step toward the other, if Charmides served that purpose for Socrates, Beatrice served that purpose for Dante. I bring up these ideas because they show how far apart Western thought is from Eastern, Socrates from Confucius. "I have never seen anyone who loves virtue as much as he loves beautiful woman," said Confucius (*Analects* 9:18, 15:13). It never occurred to him, or to the average sensual man anywhere in the world, that desire for a woman could lead to a desire for virtue and the beauty of the universe.

Now let me turn to the actual teaching methods. Confucius, so keen to learn and so learned, yet professed to know nothing about spirits and, occasionally, even much about men and their affairs. This attitude encouraged students to admit their own ignorance. It shouldn't be difficult to say, "I don't know," when Confucius himself did so from time to time. Confucius sometimes formulated an idea in the form of a question, thus stimulating his students to think. He was also far more open to his students' answers—their views—than were teachers of his time.

Nevertheless, the dominant Confucian method of teaching was to dispense wisdom from above.

Socrates went much further in both his profession of ignorance and in his resorting to the technique of questioning. When the oracle of Apollo declared Socrates to be the wisest of men, Socrates sought to disprove the oracle by finding men wiser than he. Failure to find them made him realize the oracular declaration's true meaning, namely, that he was wise because he at least knew the depth of his ignorance concerning the sort of knowledge that really mattered, which was what "good" meant and how one was to conduct one's life so as to become good.

The questioning (dialectical) technique that Socrates used forced the student to be aware of his own ignorance and from that low point rise, by gradual steps, toward knowledge. However, the technique could numb a student. "Numbed as though by a stingray" was how Meno put it. To Meno's complaint and, particularly, to his use of the stingray analogy, Socrates replied: "If the stingray paralyzes others only through being paralyzed itself, then the comparison is just, but not otherwise. It is not that, knowing the answer myself, I perplex other people. The truth is rather that I infect them with the perplexity I feel myself."[15] To another student, Theaetetus, who complained of dizziness from the endless probing, Socrates said that this uncomfortable state was the beginning of wisdom.

The danger of the Socratic method lay in making the disoriented student feel drawn to nihilistic despair, to think that philosophy was just a game, played in the manner of Sophists. This danger was averted because Socrates taught by example as well as by argument. He inspired a desire for goodness in the young by manifesting his own goodness both in his actions and, notwithstanding the ceaseless probing, in "the excellence of his conversation about virtue and human affairs in general."[16] Moreover, Socrates could never descend to game-playing, for he was not only a good man but also a deeply serious, religious man whose idea of "Good" came from a source that is out of this world.[17]

To recapitulate some of Socrates' outstanding qualities: He exemplified courage and patience, simplicity and self-control. He embraced poverty as a condition for attaining wisdom and seldom let go a chance to remind his followers of the second-rateness of wealth and power. Sensual to a high degree, he never allowed his lower nature to override his duties to the young and to his own psyche or soul. He seemed not to know anger or hatred, as the following story shows. One day, someone who was arguing with him ran out of arguments and gave Socrates a slap in the face. Socrates replied quietly, "It is very annoying not to know when one ought to put on a helmet before going out."[18] Ever searching for truth, which always seemed to elude his grasp, he was nevertheless a relaxed figure, at ease with himself and the world. He enjoyed banquets and reveling with his companions, he drank hard, and yet he was never drunk. Out of his sense of duty to the state he accepted the death sentence for sedition even though he denied the charge and even though he could have easily escaped the penalty with the connivance of his friends. The wisdom that Socrates disclaimed for himself was recognized as his by his contemporaries. When the governor of the prison bade Socrates farewell he called him the "bravest, gentlest, best" man who had ever been under his charge; and Plato ended his account of the death scene with the words: "Hereupon Crito closed his eyes and mouth, and so ended our friend, the man we hold the best and most upright of his age."

As for posterity's view of Socrates, besides the outstanding virtues already noted, certain common touches paradoxically enhance his aura of greatness. These touches came to the fore as he prepared for death. For example, not needing consolation himself, he yet sought to console his young friends with the argument that the soul survived the body to share in the eternity of truth and goodness that it knew. He reconciled with his wife, bidding her and their two teenaged children a long farewell. Considerate of others to the last, Socrates washed his own body so that others would not have to perform the office upon a corpse. And his last words were not a high-sounding peroration but rather the plain, "Crito, we owe a cock to Asclepius; do not forget to pay the debt."[19]

Wolfgang Amadeus Mozart (1756–1791)

Closer to our time, we are more likely to have complete biographies—at least, facts of various kind spread over a person's life span. This is true of Mozart and Keats, the next two good people I would like to introduce. Both died young—Mozart at age thirty-five and Keats even younger, at only twenty-five. And so if we miss the childhood and youth of Confucius and Socrates, we feel a sense of incompletion in the lives of Mozart and Keats. What if they had lived to middle age? We can't help wondering at the miracles of music and poetry they surely would have produced, for these two were at the peak of their powers when they died. They themselves had a sense of incompletion. Keats's last poem was about his hands, so capable of doing good work, turning icy cold in death; and Mozart struggled, unsuccessfully, to complete his Requiem on his deathbed.

Mozart and Keats were geniuses. Were they also good people? We are in the habit of restricting "good" to a rather narrow moral sense when we apply it to human beings. A good person is a kind person, someone who helps his or her neighbors, someone who does good deeds. But cannot a supreme work of art also be considered a good deed? Mozart's good deeds are his music, Keats's good deeds are his poetry. We who benefit from them are glad that these artists once walked the earth, as we are glad that saints once walked the earth. But this is not all. I see another sense to the word "good" that allows me to include not only geniuses but also babies, children, and superb athletes in the pantheon. And this is the sense that God used when he looked down upon his creation and called it "good." Babies are good even if they have yet to do a good deed. Superb athletes are good even if they do not religiously tithe. Mental giants are good even if they don't sell all they possess for the sake of the poor. There is something about them—their beauty, vitality, or genius—that makes us smile in appreciation and gratitude, that makes us feel more fully alive. But this can only be true if their personalities are not, in other ways, deeply flawed.

We appreciate Mozart for his musical genius. But if he is to be true to his middle name, Amadeus ("Beloved of God"), God's favor has to reach further than a single talent. What can we say about Mozart as a human being? What was he like? Very early in life Mozart showed remarkable powers of concentration. He was totally absorbed in whatever occupied him at the time. Learning arithmetic at age three, he proceeded to cover table, chairs, and walls with numbers and could forget even music! As for music, he learned a minuet and trio "one day before his fifth birthday in half an hour at half past nine in the evening of January 26, 1761," boasted Mozart's proud father, Leopold. Mozart also demon-strated concentration and discipline when he taught himself to play the violin before he was seven years old, and he soon played it well enough to perform as a soloist in public. Children do become deeply engaged in whatever activity captures their attention. That's one of their endearing qualities—this love of the world and the need to plunge into it. Mozart clearly had this love and this need more than most.[20]

Love of the world is indicated in various ways. One is simply the love of travel. Mozart traveled far and wide for professional reasons, but, despite the harsh conditions of the road, he clearly took pleasure to be on it. On his way to Italy in June 1779 he wrote to his mother: "Dearest Mama! My heart is completely enchanted with all these pleasures, because it is so jolly on this journey, because it is so warm in the carriage and because our coachman is a fine fellow who, when the road gives him the slightest chance, drives so fast." From Naples he wrote: "I too am still alive and always merry as usual and I simply love traveling." And from Bologna: "I have a great desire to ride a donkey." One admitted failing, curious in one who liked to travel, was his almost total indifference to landscape and nature. Even Vesuvius did not elicit more comment than that "[it] is smoking furiously today." But then, Mozart admitted in a letter to his father when he was twenty-one years old, "I cannot write poetically, for I am no poet. I cannot artfully arrange my phrases so as to give light and shade. Neither am I a painter; nor can I even express my thoughts by gesture and pantomime, for I am no dancer. But I can do so in sounds. I am a musician."[21]

Mozart was partial to finery, a taste he probably first acquired when, as a child prodigy, he hobnobbed with royalty and the princes of the church. There is a portrait of him, age six, in a gala dress given him by the Empress Maria Theresa. He felt a need to be seen as their social equal, which to him meant wearing fine clothes and being driven around in a carriage. But he also took an innocent delight in things—a new watch, a red coat with gold buttons, a billiard table, a household pet, or just a glass of fine champagne—and in such commonplaces of life as a daily walk in the Augarten in Vienna, a day in the country, an evening at whist, a game of billiards, devising tough riddles, and telling risqué jokes.[22]

Mozart's playfulness is amply shown in his letters to his sister, Nannerl. At age fifteen he wrote to her: "That reminds me. Have you heard what happened here? I will tell you. We left Count Firmian's today to go home and when we reached our street, we opened the hall door and what do you think we did? Why, we went in. Farewell my little lung. I kiss you my liver, and remain as always my stomach. Your unworthy brother Wolfgang. Please, please, dear sister, something is biting me. Do come and scratch me." He wrote her letters in which he switched, sometimes in a single sentence, from Italian to German to English and even to

Latin. He punned shamelessly, invented words to make nonsense rhymes, and wrote alternate lines upside down. One feels in him a volcanic mental energy that had to break down the stately sentences of language and make of it a game—an occasion for all sorts of inventiveness, except ones of beauty and sublimity, which, of course, Mozart reserved for music.

Mozart craved affection all his life and was also more than happy to give it. As a little boy Mozart kept asking people whether they loved him, and when they playfully said no, the boy, though fond of jokes and pranks himself, would break down and cry. There are stories of him jumping into the Hapsburg empress's lap, putting his arms around her neck, and earnestly kissing her, hoping for a like response. When Mozart was twenty-two years old, his father reminded him of his affectionate ways as a boy. "You never went to bed without standing on a chair and singing to me *Oragna fiagata fa,* and ending by kissing me again and again on the tip of my nose." On the road he sent his mother ten thousand or even a billion kisses. He was full of praise and affection for his sister, also a child prodigy. "I have been quite astonished that you can compose so beautifully," he wrote to his sister from Rome in 1770, acknowledging receipt of a song she had sent him. He addressed his sister as "Carissima sorella mia" or as "allerliebste Schwester." Repeatedly, he assured her of his love and asked, in return, to "aimez-moi toujours."[23]

He strove to maintain a fond, filial relationship with his father under the most difficult of circumstances, for his father was a monster of love, at times so tender that he could break into tears upon hearing his son's new string quartet, at other times coldly controlling and calculating. In 1773, when Mozart was fully an adult, he wrote pleadingly to his father: "Allow me only one request, and that is, not to think so ill of me."[24] Perhaps Mozart's most fulfilling experience of love was with his wife, Constanze. Constanze was enough of a musician to fully appreciate her husband's genius, but, more importantly, both she and Mozart were playful and physically passionate. They could enjoy each other in music, in society, and in bed. In a letter to his wife dated 5 July 1791, he wrote: "My one wish is that my affairs were settled, so that I could be with you again. You would never believe how long the time seems to me since I left you! I cannot describe my feelings to you—there is a kind of emptiness which hurts me sharply—a kind of longing, never ceasing, because never satisfied. . . . When I think how merry we were together in Baden—like children! And what sad, weary hours I live through here! Even my work gives me no joy, because I am accustomed to break off from time to time and exchange a few words with you, and that pleasure is now, alas, impossible."[25]

Human love invariably contains a tragic element, if only because its intensity cannot be sustained, and, moreover, it is almost always asymmetrical—that is, one partner is more loving and needy than the other. For all Mozart's desire to love and be loved, his ventures of the heart all seem to have ended on an ambiguous or downbeat note. Except for periods through childhood, Mozart's relationship with his father was turbulent. In his relationship with his mother there was an element of guilt. When she died he "wished at that moment to depart with her," as though to compensate for his neglect of her in life. For reasons as yet unclear—though it might have been sibling rivalry raising its ugly head after the death of both parents—the mutual affection of brother and sister cooled in the last years of his life. And in these last years even his loving relationship with Constanze showed signs of strain.

Familial and marital love places heavy demands on luck, including the luck of possessing a sunny nature. Friendship is more within human reach. Universally seen as desirable, the ability to share the world with another is in itself a measure of virtue. Mozart had a talent for friendship. In his midteens he sought it with two boys, the gifted young Giuseppe Maria Pallavicini in Bologna and the English violin prodigy Thomas Linley in Florence. Linley was accidentally drowned in his twenty-first year. Mozart never forgot him and always mentioned his name when, years later, he met English society in Vienna. In the last years of his life, in

Vienna, Mozart assuaged his loneliness and dark moods in the tender company of people his own age or younger. He was particularly close to Gottfried von Jacquin, son of a famous botanist. Jacquin, his sister Franziska, who was also Mozart's pupil, and others of like mind formed a group that gathered weekly for discussions, games, and music making. In Mozart's souvenir album Jacquin wrote in April 1787: "True genius without heart is a thing of naught—for not great understanding alone, not imagination alone, nor both together, make genius—Love! Love! That is the soul of genius." Mozart wrote a song for Jacquin in November 1787 and attached to it the words: "If the song in question is necessary to prove my friendship for you, you have no further cause to doubt it, for here it is. But I trust that even *without this song* you are convinced of my true friendship." Several songs by Mozart were published with his friend's name on them, and Mozart even encouraged his friend to use one of these songs for courtship.[26]

Generosity came to Mozart effortlessly. Friedrich Rochlitz, a Leipzig editor, thought it excessive. "How much he worked out of pure kindness for merely acquaintances! How much more for his friends! How often did he sacrifice himself for poor traveling virtuosos! . . . How often did he share bed and board, etc. with them, if they came without money and acquaintances in Vienna." Here is one of the many stories of his generosity that was in circulation.

"Dear old man," said Mozart, "what do I owe you for your efforts? Tomorrow I leave here."

The old man, who was constantly embarrassed, stuttered: "Your imperial majesty—I'd like to say—Your imperial majesty, Sir Kapellmeister—I have indeed been here on several different occasions—I ask nevertheless—one Thaler—"

"One Thaler? That is not enough to pay such a good man, even for only one visit." And thereupon he pressed into his hand several ducats.[27]

Mozart was conspicuously indifferent to politics. During the last two years of his life, between 1789 and 1791, Europe was convulsed by the French Revolution, and yet not once did he mention it in his abundant correspondence. This is all the more strange when we know that Mozart was consumed by a sense of fairness, of justice, and could flare up into white-hot anger against those who misused power. He had scant respect for people of rank. He lived too close to archbishops and archdukes, emperors and empresses, to be taken in. It would never have occurred to him to admire Napoleon, as Beethoven did before he saw the tyrant beneath the mask of social revolutionary.

Mozart himself was a revolutionary, and not only in music. His radical temperament was expressed, however, in personal behavior rather than in organized politics. One aspect of Mozart's behavior that has drawn much attention from his biographers was his scatological excess. True, in the eighteenth century people in

Mozart's social class—one that hovered between servant and re-spectable bourgeoisie—did not shy away from using crude words, and not only Mozart but his sister and cousins and even his parents were quite free with them. However, they did so with nothing like the total frankness and exuberance of Mozart. Mo-zart, it would seem, wanted to remind people of their fundamen-tal equality in bodily functions and sexual urges, that sitting on the throne one still sat on one's ass, that during the politest min-uet danced in the most gorgeous salon one couldn't help being aware—if one were honest—of tumescent breasts and groins. Mozart was a prankster who enjoyed the social disruption and role reversals of the carnival. He embodied the spirit of radical unrest—the "carnivalesque"—a term that the modern Russian critic Mikhail Bakhtin popularized.

There was, of course, much more than nose-thumbing high spirits. There was also compassion. In the opera *Don Giovanni* Mozart dug deep into the dark heart of the villainous Don, a man who was totally selfish, beyond redemption, and swallowed by the flames of hell at the end of the opera. Yet Mozart redeemed him by giving him beautiful music. There was equality. We are all equal in our biological needs, and we are all equal in the eyes of God. In *Die Zauberflöte* we can have two social unequals—the princess Pa-mina and the woodsman Papageno—sing a love duet. "High" and "low" styles, snobbishly kept apart in the musical culture of our time, collided in Mozart's operas, and never more so than in *Die Zauberflöte*. Lastly, Mozart narrowed the distinction, as did Bach before him, between sacred and secular. The breathtaking soprano in the Agnus Dei of the Coronation Mass anticipates Countess Almaviva's aria "Dove sono" in *Le Nozze di Figaro*. Mozart seemed to have believed that human beings, in their yearning, cannot distinguish between the Divine Beloved and the Human Beloved.

High-spirited, sexually frank, politically antiestablishment, in actual behavior Mozart strove for respectability, so much so that he could seem almost bourgeois. "I like to be merry, but be assured," he said to his father, "that I can be grave despite everyone." He claimed to be shocked by the language and behavior of the people he encountered in Salzburg and elsewhere. Religion served him as a moral ballast. "I know myself well enough to be sure that I have enough religion never at any time to do what I could not do openly before all the world; but the mere idea of traveling alone in the society of people whose way of thinking is so different from my own (and from that of all honorable people) frightens me." He had his needs but did not want to live a dissipated life. "The voice of nature speaks as loud in me as in others. . . . [But] I cannot possibly live as do most young men in these days. In the first place, I have too much religion; in the second place, I have too great a love of my neighbor, and am too honorably-minded to seduce an innocent maiden; while, in the third place, I have too much horror and disgust, too much fear and loathing of disease, and too much care for my health, to consort with whores."[28]

In December 1784 Mozart joined the Freemasons. It was not really a political move, for the Masonic lodges of Vienna were essentially social clubs and talking shops, producing ideas that led to acts of individual philanthropy rather than social reform and change on any scale. Yet the move *was* political to the extent that Mozart wished to align himself to the Enlightenment program. He yearned for a pure religion, shorn of all superstition, flourishing in a world of equality and universal brotherhood, in short, a utopia. Mozart might have found some consolation in the fellowship of his Masonic brothers, but it is doubtful that he seriously believed in the actualization of Masonic ideals.

Mozart needed friends, needed the warmth and support of like-minded people. Confident of his gifts and brimming with high spirits, he yet succumbed to periodic attacks of depression and melancholy. On 31 July 1778, in the aftermath of his mother's death, he wrote, "I often wonder whether life is worth living. . . . I am neither hot nor cold—and don't find much pleasure in anything." After a lackluster tour of Berlin he said to his friend Michael Puchberg in the spring of 1790, "For some time you must have noticed my constant sadness." Later that year he wrote to Constanze: "If people could see into my heart, I should almost feel ashamed. To me everything is cold as ice. Perhaps if you were with me I might possibly take pleasure in the kindness of those I meet here. But, as it is, everything seems so empty."[29]

A just society may well be an unrealizable dream, but, even if it is realized, bodily corruption and death will still remain. Mozart was haunted by death. His way of transcending it was music, the gift of a power that enabled him to transmute all he knew of life—its full range of joys and sorrows, hopes and fears, including the fear of death—into the beauty of sound. Salvation lay in this beauty, to which he had had access since childhood. As he matured and his experiences of good and evil deepened, his music followed a similar path of greater maturity and depth. Mozart experimented with the widest range of musical genres, returning to some periodically as he gained new insight into means of expression. "In his last year," Maynard Solomon writes, "he returned to some of the earlier sources of his strength—to the piano concerto, to German-language opera, to church music (the *Ave verum corpus* K. 618 and the Requiem) and to Masonic music (two cantatas and *Die Zauberflöte*), all of which had been absent from his musical workshop for from three to ten years. The return to church music . . . connotes a renewal of faith, a desire for grace, an appeal for relief from pain, and even an offer of expiation or repentance."[30] And surely it also connotes an affirmation in the power of sound to stall the inroads of death, for sound *is* life and, infinitely more so, sound of divine beauty.

Mozart's genius astonished all those who knew him. The aged Goethe, who as a young man had heard the seven-year-old boy play in Frankfurt, considered him to be "unreachable" in music, on a level with Raphael and Shakespeare in their domains. To Goethe it was ridiculous to say that Mozart composed *Don Giovanni*. "Composition! As if it were a piece of cake or biscuit, which had been stirred together out of eggs, flour, and sugar!" No, it was more like a spiritual creation or obedience to a higher order. Joseph Haydn told Mozart's father "before God and as an honest man" that his son was "the greatest composer" he knew "either in person or by name." In 1881 Johannes Brahms remarked to a friend, "Every number in Mozart's *Figaro* is a miracle to me; I find it absolutely incomprehensible how someone can create something so absolutely perfect."[31] The composer Ferruccio Busoni said: "There are bad composers, there are competent composers, there are good composers, there are great composers—and there is Mozart." The theologian Karl Barth said that angels might play Bach to praise God, but by themselves they played Mozart.[32] The conductor Daniel Barenboim said that he felt Mozart's Symphony no. 41 ("Jupiter") included everything one could ask of music. And so from Mozart's own lifetime to the year 2006, the 250th anniversary of his birth, people were and continue to be astonished. Encomiums continue to pour in. They come from experts and professionals in music, but they also come from ordinary listeners like myself who, whether attending a concert or unexpectedly hearing a Mozart aria from an open window, feel that they too have been touched by God, that their middle name is also Amadeus.

John Keats (1795–1821)

Near the end of his life, in a twelve-month period from mid-September 1818 to mid-September 1819, Keats wrote almost all of his greatest poetry—poetry that adorns the English language and is beloved as Mozart's music is beloved, that is, with astonishment and gratitude. Both died young, and that itself creates an image of genius, of men whose works are not belabored but are, rather, gifts. Both came from a modest social background, both had to struggle for financial security, the one dependent on the goodwill of aristocratic patrons, the other on the goodwill of publishers and clients. Both had a vivacious, even pugnacious personality, and both enjoyed life in all its richness and range. Both liked to joke and used language that could be coarse. True, Mozart went much further in that direction, but then he was a man of the less inhibited eighteenth century, whereas Keats consciously culti-vated good manners of the sort considered desirable in his and a later time. Both were deeply attached to their family. Both em-braced rational thought and had no patience for anything super-stitious. Keats, for example, was an admirer of Voltaire. On the other hand, both were religious, though not followers of orthodox doctrine and practice. Both detested the social hierarchies of their day, and both were politically liberal. In May 1819, when Keats was already quite sick, he even thought of fighting in the wars of liberation that were at that time raging in Chile. Both admired the music of Haydn. Both not only were geniuses but were also good men.

However, there were important differences. Mozart was a child prodigy, Keats was not. Mozart composed two short pieces for clavier at age five and his first full-scale opera, *La finta semplice,* at age twelve. At age twelve Keats was still a rather rowdy schoolboy, more eager to pick a fight than to hit the books. In his midteens he began to show an interest in literature. Once literature, especially poetry, took hold, it became for him a passion. But, so far as we know, Keats was already eighteen when he composed his first poem—a work imitative of Spenser. And he was twenty-one when, in a burst of inspiration, he wrote "On First Looking into Chapman's Homer" in one evening. It is generally considered to be his first truly original and masterful work. Even as a small child Mozart was acclaimed and adored by the greatest musicians and literary figures of his time as well as by prelates, emperors, and empresses. Keats, by contrast, received high, unadulterated praise mostly from his friends, and he has always had powerful detractors in publishers and journal editors who don't like his liberal political viewpoint. As for poets, such luminaries as Byron, Shelley, and Wordsworth gave only qualified praise. Mozart's sonatas and chamber music appeal to musical sophisticates, whereas his operas appeal to both sophisticates and people who simply like rousing tunes and a good story. With poetry—and not only the poetry of Keats—it is the opposite. Both sophisticated and ordinary readers may like the short pieces, but only readers of ample literary knowledge and discernment can truly appreciate book-length poems such as *Endymion*. Mozart composed for every man, Keats wrote for the discerning few. Lastly, Mozart could emerge from the shadow of his illustrious predecessors (Bach and Haydn, among others), Keats could not. All poets, no matter how talented, have to tip their hat to Shakespeare.

We do know more about the man Keats than we can ever know about the man Mozart, and the reason is that Keats communicated in words. From Keats's poetry we know the scope and depth of his sympathies, his hopes and fears. From his letters we know something else—his philosophy of literature and life, his friendships, and the sort of human being he hoped to be. Both Mozart and Keats, for all their inwardness, made friends easily and were delightful company. Both reveled in the external world. Keats's sense of wonder, his joy in seeing the world opening up before him, is captured in the poem inspired by Chapman's translation of Homer. Reading it made him feel

> like some watcher of the skies
> When a new planet swims into his ken;
> Or like stout Cortez when with eagle eyes
> He stared at the Pacific—and all his men
> Look'd at each other with a wild surmise—
> Silent, upon a peak in Darien.

The poem "On the Sea" keeps up this feeling of awe in the presence of vast terrestrial nature—the sea that "keeps eternal whispering around / Desolate shores, and with its mighty swell / Gluts twice ten thousand caverns."

But it is in the small things and events of life that Keats's wonderment reached the peak of voluptuousness.

> O for a beaker full of the warm South,
> Full of the true, the blushful Hippocrene,
> With beaded bubbles winking at the brim,
> And purple-stained mouth;
> That I might drink and leave the world unseen,
> And with thee fade away into the forest dim.
>
> "Ode to a Nightingale"

He wrote of autumn as the "season of mists and mellow fruitfulness" that conspires with "the maturing sun"

> To bend with apples the moss'd cottage-trees,
> And fill all fruit with ripeness to the core;
> To swell the gourd, and plump the hazel shells
> With a sweet kernel;
> To set budding more,

> And still more, later flowers for the bees
> Until they think warm days will never cease,
> For Summer has o'er-brimm'd their clammy cells.
>
> "To Autumn"

That's outdoors. Indoors, Keats drew our attention to the mouth-watering delights of artfully prepared nature—to food.

> While he from forth the closet brought a heap
> Of candied apple, quince, and plum, and gourd;
> With Jellies soother than the creamy curd,
> And lucent syrops, tinct with cinnamon;
> Manna and dates, in argosy transferr'd
> From Fez, and spiced dainties, every one,
> From silken Samarcand to cedar'd Lebanon.
>
> "The Eve of St. Agnes"[33]

And, oh, the pleasure of eating a nectarine! "I [am] writing with one hand," he wrote to a friend, "and with the other holding to my Mouth a Nectarine—good god how fine. It went down soft, slushy, oozy—all its delicious embonpoint melted down my throat like a beatified Strawberry."[34]

Human beings are more difficult to love. Keats loved them nonetheless—his family and his friends. Keats lost his father at age eight and his mother at age fifteen. Very little is known about his father, and it is astonishing that Keats nowhere mentions him in his letters. His mother suffered ill health and eventually succumbed to tuberculosis. In her last two years of life Keats appointed himself her principal nurse. Years later, the painter Benjamin Haydon wrote in his diary: "He sat up whole nights in a great chair, would suffer nobody to give her medicine but himself, and even cooked her food; he did all, & read novels in her intervals of ease." Keats's brief career as an apothecary and an assistant to the surgeon at Guy's Hospital probably had its beginning there. Throughout his life his concern for others was physical and material as well as intellectual and spiritual.

At fifteen Keats considered himself the head of his family, which included George, Tom, and Fanny. George was a robust child who needed little care. Only much later in life, when George was married and immigrated with his wife, Georgiana, to America, did Keats show the depth of his affection for his brother and his wife, whom he called sister, in poems and letters.

> Now I direct my eyes into the west,
> Which at this moment is in sunbeams drest:
> Why westward turn? 'Twas but to say adieu!
> 'Twas but to kiss my hand, dear George, to you!

In a letter to George, Keats reported on Tom's declining health. He said the bad news must be told and that "you must, my dear brother and sister, take example from me and bear up against any calamity for my sake as I do for yours. Ours are ties which prevent the deleterious effects of one great, solitary grief. I have Fanny and I have you—the three people whose happiness to me is sacred."[35]

Is it possible to feel close to people on the other side of an ocean? Keats thought so. "Now the reason why I do not feel at the present moment so far from you is that I remember your ways and manners and actions; I know your manner of thinking, your manner of feeling: I know what shape your joy or your sorrow would take; I know the manner of you walking, standing, sauntering, sitting down, laughing, punning, and every action so truly that you seem near to me. You will remember me in the same manner—and the more when I tell you that I shall read a passage of Shakespeare every Sunday at ten o'clock—you read one at the same time and we shall be as near each other as blind bodies can be in the same room."[36]

Fanny, the sister, was Keats's junior by eight years. He acted toward her as protector and guide. When she was fourteen he wrote: "We have been so little together since you have been able to reflect on things that I know not whether you prefer the History of King Pepin to Bunyan's Pilgrims Progress—or Cinderella and her glass slipper to Moor's Almanack. . . . You must tell me all you read if it be only six pages in a week. This I feel as a necessity: for we ought to become intimately acquainted, in order that I may not only, as you grow up, love you as my only sister, but confide in you as my dearest friend." He could tease. He sent her a lighthearted poem and wrote, "My dear Fanny, I am ashamed of writing you such stuff, nor would I if it were not for being tired after my day's walking, and ready to tumble into bed so fatigued that when I am asleep you might sew my nose to my great toe and trundle me round the town like a hoop without waking me." Fanny's official guardian was Richard Abbey, a London merchant. Keats and his sister were not often together, partly because Fanny could not travel without her guardian's permission, which, for one reason or another, he sometimes refused to grant. Keats sought to reassure his sister. "We have been very little together: but you have not the less been with me in thought. You have no one in the world besides me who would sacrifice any thing for you—I feel myself the only protector you have. In all your little troubles, think of me with the thought that there is at least one person in England who, if he could, would help you out of them. I live in hopes of being able to make you happy."[37]

Without doubt, Tom, because of his ill health, drew most on Keats's scarce resources of time, energy, and money. He made ambitious plans of sending his brother to a sunnier climate—he thought of Lisbon—but had to settle on English towns instead. He accompanied Tom to the seaside resort of Margate, and there the two of them walked, lolled on the grass hilltops, saw plays, and read Wordsworth's poetry in the two-volume edition that Keats brought with him. They were again together at Canterbury. All the while Keats felt the pull of London, the society of his literary friends, and, above all, the need to answer his poetic calling, which became increasingly urgent as Keats began to suspect that he himself might be afflicted by the disease (tuberculosis) that killed his mother. The depth of his yearning for quiet, untroubled living—for normality—is captured in the following poem, addressed to his brothers, on the occasion of Tom's seventeenth birthday.

> Small, busy flames play through the fresh-laid coals
> And their faint cracklings o'er our silence creep
> Like whispers of the household gods that keep
> A gentle empire o'er fraternal souls,
> And while, for rhymes, I search around the poles,
> Your eyes are fix'd, as in poetic sleep,
> Upon the lore so voluble and deep,
> That aye at fall of night our care condoles.
> This is your birth-day, Tom, and I rejoice
> That thus it passes smoothly, quietly.
> Many such eves of gently whispering noise
> May we together pass, and calmly try
> What are this world's true joys—ere the great voice
> From its fair face shall bid our spirits fly.[38]

Tom died six days after his nineteenth birthday, nursed by his brother through the last month of his life, during which he slipped in and out of feverish dreams and coughed up phlegm specked with blood. Keats was depressed and worn out but also scared, for the medical lore of his time asserted that anyone who spent long hours in the room of a dying consumptive was liable to come down with the same disease.

Keats, though not especially sociable as a child, actively sought the company of others once he reached his late teens and had taken wholeheartedly to literature and poetry. From others—almost all of whom were older—he counted on knowledge, inspiration, and love. These were freely given, from which we may conclude that Keats himself gave freely, that his genial temperament and outstanding talent drew people to him. Keats had a vocation for friendship. Benjamin Bailey, whom Keats met for the first time in the summer of 1817, recollected that during their time together "there was no reserve of any kind between us" and insisted that he was able to "throw light on Keats's youthful genius and character" because "the dew and freshness of youthful trustfulness was upon each of us." Benjamin Haydon, the artist, was another close friend. In May 1817 Keats wrote, "I am very sure that you [Haydon] do love me as your own brother—I have seen it in your continual anxiety for me—and I assure you that your welfare and fame is and will be a chief pleasure to me all my life." Haydon was sick and in need of money the following year. Though financially strapped himself, Keats offered help. Haydon replied: "Keats! Upon my soul I could have wept at your letter; to find one of real heart & feeling is to me a blessed solace. . . . I declare to God I do not feel alone in the world now you have written me that letter. . . . Dear Keats—I believe you from my soul when you say you would sacrifice all for me; and when your means are gone, if

God gives me means, my heart & house & every thing shall be shared with you."[39]

Such closeness and intensity inevitably generated tension and misunderstanding. Keats showed his awareness of the problem when he made a distinction between "pastoral friendship" to correspond with the "cold pastoral" in poetry, which gives pleasure like a cool breeze on a hot day, and "tragic friendship" to correspond with the sort of poetry to which Keats aspired, poetry that elevates and depresses, gives one glimpses of heaven only to have them withdrawn. Much as he enjoyed society, in his depressed moods Keats couldn't help feeling that people liked him because he made a point of hiding his talent so that, as he put it, "they can all show to advantage in a room." To Charles Brown, the last close friend he made, he offered the advice of greater selfishness—an advice he no doubt was also giving himself. "You have been living for others more than any man I know. This is a vexation to me, because it has been depriving you, in the very prime of your life, of pleasures which it was your duty to procure." A few months later he wrote Brown again to say, "I cannot answer anything in your letter, which followed me from Naples to Rome, because I am afraid to look it over again. I am so weak (in mind) that I cannot bear the sight of any handwriting of a friend I love so much as I do you."[40]

Keats might have preached selfishness, but he couldn't have been a successful practitioner, for how, other than with the draw of his own exemplary behavior, could he retain such loyal friends? Keats went to Rome with the hope that the kindlier climate there would alleviate his fevers, stomach pains, and coughing. Joseph Severn, a rising young painter, accompanied him and became, in effect, his nurse through the months that Keats's health steadily declined. Keats worried that his "lingering death" would ruin Severn's career prospects and also that his friend, never having witnessed death before, might not know how severely his patience would be tried, since it was not a pretty sight to see "continued diarrhea," and that he ran the risk of catching the disease. Severn was indeed shocked and reported to Charles Brown, their mutual friend, that he had not dreamed of "THIS" in London. Yet he stayed. Day after day, he lit the fire, cooked Keats's breakfast, made his bed, swept the room, and read to him. At around eleven o'clock in the evening of 23 February 1821 Keats died in his arms.

What sort of man was Keats? Poets are supposed to be wild, emotionally high-strung, and unstable. Keats, however, was eminently sane and stable. As evidence, I offer his way of maintaining balance, of keeping his mind occupied and focused when he grew "vapourish." "I rouse myself," he wrote his brother George, "wash and put on a clean shirt, brush my hair and clothes, tie my shoe-strings neatly . . . and then all clean and comfortable I sit down to write." That, in my view, is sound advice to all of us when we feel antsy and out of sorts. To be sane—normal, even ordinary—may not seem much of a virtue until we remember that "sane" is another word for "whole" or "holy."

Keats wanted to do good. He said that over and over again in his letters. To do good meant helping his fellow human beings, protesting against injustice, and fighting for the cause of freedom. But he always knew that, for him, doing good must mean first and foremost developing his poetic gift to the full. The product of that gift was what he uniquely had to offer the world. Put thus, Keats sounds like an egotist. Was he one? Like many accomplished people, he was and wasn't. Keats's sunny confidence in himself, his enormous drive, and his ability to focus on his work to the exclusion of everything else might be taken as marks of an egotist. Yet he strongly believed that to be a good poet he must empty himself to the extent of losing his own identity. A word he liked to use when he disapproved of a work was that it was "egotistical." Keats, who admired Wordsworth, nevertheless had reservations, the primary one being Wordsworth's tendency to impose a preconceived pattern of value on reality. He admired Shakespeare without reservation because Shakespeare seemed to lack a self: the world in all its richness and complexity flowed through him as ink through a quill. A good poet must be selfless, and selflessness is the quality that defines a good person.

Selflessness alone does not, of course, make a poet. Something else is required—capability. "Negative capability" is how Keats put it. The mind must be at work: there must be imagination and knowledge. "Negative" is that openness that invites the world to enter; "capability" is the mind that sorts out, intensifies, and ponders over the meaning of that which enters. Keats set himself an impossible task: he wanted both concrete experience and abstraction, both the sensual richness of the world and its metaphysical significance. In this regard, he was more ambitious than Plato, for whom he had otherwise an affinity. Plato's ideal was easier to attain, since he believed that one could and should abandon the sensual in favor of abstract essence as one moved up the ladder of perfection. Keats wanted to hold on to both, if not in his life, then in his poetry.

Openness has another consequence. It makes one aware of the ubiquity and power of evil. Allowing such awareness to enter one's life threatens its balance, sanity, and wholeness. Besides knowing that humans can be grossly self-centered, greedy, vain, cruel, and morally obtuse is the further and darker knowledge that all living things are engaged in a struggle for survival. Keats predated Darwin, but primitive Darwinian ideas were already in the air in his time. Keats himself observed that "not only the hawk, but also the robin" are predatory. Creatures strive for their moment under the sun by killing other creatures only in turn to be killed themselves. In any case, death awaits all.

In life, misunderstandings can be corrected, distances and separation can be overcome. Death is the ultimate separation and dissolution, the distance that cannot be overcome. Death obsessed Keats in life and in his poetry. "Here, where men sit and hear each other groan; / Where palsy shakes a few, sad, last grey hairs; / Where youth grows pale, and spectre-thin, and dies." (The youth referred to here is his brother Tom.) Life entails death, as does sexual passion, life at its highest emotional pitch. Sexual passion is death in its climax of swooning oblivion, in its deep frustrations and disappointments, and in the way it negates life's other ventures, first and foremost of which, for Keats, is poetry.

> She took me to her elfin grot
> And there she wept and sigh'd full sore,
> And there I shut her wild wild eyes
> With kisses four.
> And there she lulled me asleep
> And there I dream'd—Ah! Woe betide!
> On the cold hill side.
> I saw pale kings and Princes too,
> Pale warriors, death pale were they all;
> They cried "La belle dame sans merci
> Thee hath in thrall."[41]

Throughout his adult life Keats denounced organized religion. On his deathbed Severn read him passages from Jeremy Taylor's

Holy Living and Holy Dying. Keats found comfort and satisfaction in the sonorous prose but could not accept its message of salvation. At times, Keats's bitterness at his approaching end when he had just hit his poetic stride made him restless and irritable. In the last few days, however, he attained a sort of peace. He told Severn that "the spring was always enchantment to me . . . perhaps the only happiness I have had in the world has been the silent growth of flowers." Interestingly, he mentioned spring rather than autumn, the season he celebrated at the height of his powers as uniquely emblematic of the human state. Keats gave instructions for his burial and urged that his headstone be inscribed with a broken lyre and the words, "Here lies one whose name was writ in water." The words are the translation of a Greek proverb and do not signify despair. Rather, Keats meant that his poetry had come to him "as naturally as leaves to a tree" and that as naturally it returned to nature.[42]

Albert Schweitzer (1875–1965)

From the 1970s onward there has been an increasing concern in the Western world for the welfare of animals and for animal rights, itself a development from, first, the civil rights movement of the 1950s and 1960s and, then, the environmental movement that quickly followed. The environmental and animal rights movements have their extreme advocates. One hears of "tree huggers," a derogatory term tagged on to people who ardently seek to protect vegetation in natural areas, and of animal righters who may use violence against institutions and scientists that do experiments on animals. These two closely linked movements, being political and centered on action, seldom bother to defend their positions philosophically and morally. Such defense can seem to them both unnecessary and a waste of time. Yet if they want a philosophical defender, they do not have to look far back in time, for there is Albert Schweitzer.

Schweitzer was one of the most accomplished men of the twentieth century. He was a distinguished theologian, a musicologist and authority on Bach, an organist and a specialist in organ building, a medical doctor and medical missionary to Africa, and a philosopher. In philosophy his principal contribution lies in his idea of "reverence for life." Reverence for life, he argued, is the most elemental position that the moral human being can and must take in regard to the world, if a civilization worthy of the name is to emerge.

Schweitzer was a "good" man, if any man can be called good. He was good in his devotion to the sick of equatorial Africa, good in his dedication to equality and justice among humans everywhere, and good in his unsentimental caring of all living creatures. Tying morality with the way humans treat other living creatures is his most distinguishing mark. To place Schweitzer as a moral person and thinker, a context—however sketchy—is needed. Here it is.

Human beings are omnivores. Their capacity to digest a wide range of foods is one reason for their success in settling the earth. Of all the foods available to them, one is almost always preferred—meat. Some people, such as the Aivilik, Iglulik, and Netsilik of the Canadian Arctic, depend almost entirely on animals for food. They have to kill to survive. They have no choice. The guilt that goes with the killing is assuaged by restricting the act to absolute necessity and to performing it with propitiatory respect. The freshly killed seal, for example, should never be laid on a dirty floor, and some water should be poured into its mouth, for the animal, though dead, can still feel thirst.[43] The Nuer of the Upper Sudan are cattle herders who love their livestock. "Love" does not seem too strong a word. "When a young man's ox comes home in the evening he pets it, rubs ashes on its back, removes ticks from its belly and scrotum, and picks adherent dung from its anus. He tethers it in front of the windscreen so that he can see it if he wakes, for no sight so fills a Nuer with contentment and pride as his oxen." Nevertheless, cattle are food and a resource to the Nuer. They provide milk, meat, and blood, and their skins are a primary raw material for making the meager goods that the Nuer possess. Obtaining milk and blood from cattle presents no moral dilemma, but killing the beloved cattle for meat does present a problem that the Nuer evade by claiming to eat only the flesh of animals that have died a natural death or that have been slaughtered for ceremonial and sacrificial purposes. The Nuer are very fond of meat. On the death of a cow they declare, "The eyes and heart are sad, but the teeth and the stomach are glad."[44]

Civilized peoples kill animals on a massive scale, impersonally and routinely, in the course of which they appear to have lost, unlike so-called primitive peoples, all sense of indebtedness and guilt. Of course, there are exceptions. Stories from Western classical antiquity show some degree of concern for animals. One thinks of the Athenian boy condemned to death for tearing out the eyes of a crow and of numerous reports of horses and other draft animals put out to pasture in their old age. Above all, as evidence of civilizational sensitivity, one thinks of the teaching of the Indian religions, outstandingly, the doctrine of *ahimsā*, with its renunciation of the will to hurt or kill, dating back to the seventh century BCE. A consequence of this doctrine is that it led the Jains, Hindus, and Buddhists to feel compassion for animals and to treat them with consideration. Nevertheless, it was belief in reincarnation, not intensity of compassion, that provided the most common justification for avoiding the molestation or slaughter of animals. Moreover, kindness to an animal earned one merit to move to a higher level of incarnation in the next cycle of life.

Christianity is widely criticized for giving humans dominion over animals and for having little to say about them. The love that the New Testament preaches with such ardor and eloquence is reserved exclusively for people. Jesus took pleasure in birds and flowers and used them in his parables. On the other hand, he drove the devil into a horde of pigs and sent them tumbling over a cliff to their death. Stories of loving relationship between men and animals do exist in early Christianity: one finds them in biographies of the desert hermits and Irish monks and, outstandingly, in the life of Francis of Assisi. Francis loved animals because they were God's creatures—they had necessarily the beauty and goodness of God's handiwork. To him, it was self-evident that animals possessed rights, notably the divine dispensation of life. Lambs, nevertheless, presented a tricky problem for the saint. A story goes that Francis met a man carrying two lambs on his shoulders to be slaughtered. Francis forthwith bartered his cloak for them. But, having rescued the lambs, he was faced with the problem of their disposal. His solution, not a very satisfactory one, was to return them to the man with the request that he take care of them.[45]

Albert Schweitzer, the theologian, was keenly aware of the lack of compassion for animals in Christianity. What evidence had existed before the nineteenth century seemed to him fainthearted. True, there was Francis, and it is curious that Schweitzer did not draw more on him. Instead, prompted by his Lutheran heritage, he offered the example of Martin Luther. Luther's servant had fashioned a net in which to catch migrating birds. To show his disapproval of the practice, Luther prepared a humorous petition against it. He pretended, however, that the petition came from the birds.[46]

This is admittedly a rather trivial example. The question remains, What made Schweitzer himself feel an urgent compassion for all living things? Both his genes and his upbringing in a pious household no doubt played a part. In any case, even at an early age Schweitzer was committed to the ideals of equality and fairness, which, if one reflects on them, are also ideals of compassion, for in compassion one identifies with another and recognizes in the other one's equal. To illustrate, here are two stories. At school young Schweitzer liked to engage his fellow students in playful scuffles. One day on his way home he took on a boy taller than he and considered stronger. Nevertheless, after much push and pull and a stumble or two, Schweitzer got on top of him. The boy underneath hissed, "Darn it, if I got soup with meat twice a week as you do, I would be as strong as you are!" Henceforth, Schweitzer found meat soup loathsome. The other story involved an overcoat. One winter young Schweitzer was given one. A tailor put it on him and said, "My goodness, Albert, you will soon be a monsieur." None of Albert's classmates—mostly village boys—wore an overcoat. Albert refused to wear his. The first time he refused his father slapped his face. He refused again and again and was slapped again and again. But he stood his ground.[47]

Respect for one's superiors is a posture for survival and comes naturally to all animals, including humans. Respect for one's peers takes a little more doing. Still, it can be done, for it has obvious advantages: it makes for social pleasantness and it encourages the kind of reciprocity that benefits both parties. Respect for people below us—the poor and the handicapped—goes against the grain and must be judged supernumerary. As to respect for nonhuman creatures, in Western civilization it is rare enough to seem a divine grace and favor. Schweitzer was touched by such divine grace and favor at age seven or eight. "Heinrich Brasch and I had made ourselves rubber band slingshots with which we could shoot small pebbles. One spring Sunday during Lent he said to me, 'Come on, let's go up the Rebberg and shoot birds.' I hated this idea, but I did not contradict him for fear he might laugh at me. We approached a leafless tree in which birds . . . were singing sweetly in the morning air. Crouching like an Indian hunter, my friend put a pebble in his slingshot and took aim. Obeying his look of command, I did the same with terrible pangs of conscience and vowing to myself to miss. At that very moment the church bells began to ring out into the sunshine, mingling their chimes with the song of the birds. . . . For me, it was a voice from Heaven. I put the slingshot aside, shooed the birds away so that they were safe from my friend, and ran home. Ever since then, when the bells of Passiontide ring out into the sunshine and the naked trees, I remember, deeply moved and grateful, how on that day they rang into my heart the commandment 'Thou shalt not kill.'"[48]

Throughout his late twenties, even while Schweitzer was establishing a firm reputation as a theologian and musicologist, he struggled to come up with a concept that could serve as the keystone for his philosophical and moral thought—a concept that addressed the core questions and dilemmas all humans faced. The ideas that other thinkers offered as well as those he himself explored all seemed partial and not quite at the deepest level. One day in September 1915 in equatorial Africa the key idea came to him. Schweitzer was on a small steamer on his way to visit the ailing wife of a missionary at M'Gômô, about 160 miles upstream from Lambaréné, where his hospital was located. "Slowly we crept upstream. . . . Lost in thought I sat on the deck of the barge, struggling to find the elementary and universal concept of the ethical that I had not discovered in any philosophy. . . . Two days passed. Late on the third day, at the very moment when, at sunset, we were making our way through a herd of hippopotamuses, there flashed upon my mind, unforeseen and unsought[,] the phrase 'reverence for life.' The iron door had yielded. The path in the thicket had become visible. Now I had found my way to the principle in which affirmation of the world and ethics are joined together!"[49]

Soon after Schweitzer arrived at Lambaréné and made some headway establishing a medical mission there, war was declared. As a German national in a French colony (Gabon), Schweitzer was tagged an enemy alien. In the period from the autumn of 1917 to the summer of 1918 he was interned at various camps in France, during which his health, normally so robust, steadily declined. He suffered dysentery, could find no relief despite assorted treatments, and also developed a cyst in his rectum that made it hard for him to sit. By the time he was freed from internment and allowed to return to his home province, Alsace, he knew, personally, the struggle and pain of survival in an equatorial forest and the humiliation and pain of life in a prison camp. The sermons he gave in 1918 at Saint Nicolai Church in Strasbourg were thus far from being merely the thoughts of an armchair philosopher; they were also those of one who had recently known toil, sickness, and depression. His recent discovery of a reverence for life was to be the focus of his sermons.

> Life means strength, will coming from the abyss and sinking into it again. Life means feeling, sensitivity, suffering. And if you are absorbed in life, if you see with perceptive eyes into this enormous animated chaos of creation, it suddenly seizes you with vertigo. In everything you recognize yourself again. The beetle that lies dead in your path—it was something that lived, that

struggled for its existence like you, that rejoiced in the sun like you, that knew anxiety and pain like you. And now it is nothing more than decomposing material—as you, too, shall be sooner or later.

You walk outside and it is snowing. Carelessly you shake the snow from your sleeves. It attracts your attention: a snowflake glistens on your hand. You cannot help looking at it, whether you wish to or not. It glistens in its wonderful design; then it quivers, and the delicate needles of which it consists contract. It is no more; it has melted, dead in your hand. The flake, which fell upon your hand from infinite space, which glistened there, quivered, and died—that is you. Wherever you see life—that is you!

Nature itself knows no reverence. At every stage of life up to the level of humanity, creatures have only the will to live, to enjoy and suffer, but no capacity to share their joys and sufferings; they may have instinctive empathy but no power to put themselves into the place of another and, hence, no real sympathy and compassion. Nature teaches cruel egotism—with but one exception. In regard to their own young, animals show love and self-sacrifice even unto death. But, to a moral human being, it is horrible to know that love and sympathy have strict and narrow borders, for such borders would seem to corrode the very virtue and meaning of these sentiments.[50]

The concept "reverence for life" can have meaning only to humans. At the same time, it presents an almost impossible challenge to them. This is so because humans are biologically constituted to be carnivorous; their very teeth, so well suited to tearing animal flesh, are an invitation to the act. And, as I have already noted, in most parts of the world people prefer meat when they have a choice. Schweitzer himself only became a vegetarian late in life. Compared with people less materially advanced, civilized beings are especially adapt at not acknowledging how their body feeds on other living things. Take cooking. By calling it an art, we make it easy to forget that the "art" depends on prior slaughter and the spilling of blood. Cookbooks never bear the title *Killing and Cooking*. Schweitzer thought that if humans must eat meat, they should at least know how the killing was done so as to prevent unnecessary cruelty. "In Africa," he wrote, "where one must do all of his own slaughtering, I force myself whenever possible to be present in order to prevent unnecessary pain to the animal." He then gave the example of killing cats—a grim yet common occurrence. "If cats must be done away with, do not try to drown them and think that everything is well when they are out of sight. They may survive for hours in misery in the water. Instead, kill them yourself with a hammer blow to the head. That is your duty toward them."[51]

Our debt to animals continues to mount, for, in addition to age-old methods of exploitation, in modern times we also experiment with them so as to find cures for human diseases or ways to ease human pain. We are monsters of immorality if we do not feel a twinge of indebtedness toward our fellow creatures, yet few of us do. Few are compelled, as was Schweitzer, to put animals near the center of their ethics.[52]

The two greatest commandments, according to Jesus, are, first, you shall love the Lord your God with all your heart, and with all your soul, and with all your mind, and with all your strength, and, second, you shall love your neighbor as yourself (Mark 12:28–34). To Schweitzer, the "neighbor" of the second commandment is not only the human stranger but also the nonhuman animal. Another famous saying of Jesus is: "What you have done to one of the least of these, you have done to me" (Matthew 25:40). To Schweitzer, the "least" of these is not necessarily another human being. It could be the "worm on the hard street, onto which he has strayed by error. [He] languishes because he cannot bore into it. Put him on soft earth or in the grass!" In helping this the least of creatures, you will have obeyed God's commandment. And the proof lies, Schweitzer might say, in your momentary glow of happiness—the happiness of having done the thing that you, in your deepest nature, were created to do.

Nevertheless, Schweitzer put human beings and their welfare first. Even as a child he was aware of suffering not only among the poor and physically handicapped but even in healthy, well-to-do families—his own family, for example. Now, suffering is a complex phenomenon; there are different kinds of suffering, but one among them is relatively simple, namely, pain. Schweitzer thought it self-evident that, much as people differed in social and eco-nomic circumstance, they all knew pain; they were bound to one another in a fellowship of pain. We may share this thought, but it is one we easily put aside. Schweitzer couldn't; he felt driven—he felt called—to relieve pain. And so at age twenty-one he planned a career path for himself as follows: For the next ten years he would continue to study and teach music, theology, and philoso-phy, but at age thirty he would begin another career as a student of medicine. "On October 13, 1905, I dropped into a letter box on the avenue de la Grande Armée in Paris letters to my parents and to some of my closest friends telling them that at the beginning of the winter term I would embark on the study of medicine with the idea of later going out to equatorial Africa as a doctor."[53]

I was a student at Oxford when I first read this passage in Schweitzer's autobiography. I was astonished that a man could change the course of his life with such insouciance—all the more so because at the time I had been reading, upon the urging of Brit-ish missionaries, some of their life stories as well as those of their nineteenth-century predecessors. I read them with indignation be-cause so often they told of God-fearing Britons who, upon hearing God's call, agonized over their decision to leave civilized society for the land of the heathen Chinese. I was indignant because I be-lieved that these missionaries, most of whom came from the lower middle class, would actually lead a more pampered life in China.

What a contrast with Schweitzer! Here was a man who really had something to give up. By the time he approached thirty, Schweitzer already enjoyed a European and North American reputation. When he dropped those letters into the letter box he had already published *The Religious Philosophy of Kant* (1899), *The Mystery of the Kingdom of God* (1901), and *J. S. Bach le musicien-poète* (1905) and he was completing *The Quest of the Historical Jesus,* which was to prove to be a seminal work in historiography and theology. In one of the letters he sent that day he resigned his position as principal of the theological faculty at the University of Strasbourg. He then applied to be admitted as a student in its medical school. From preeminent professor to struggling student — such was the change in Schweitzer's status and career path. The years in medical school were difficult for him and surely all the more so because he believed at the time (though it turned out to be not quite the case) that at the end of the course he would have to give up the three things he loved doing most: playing the organ, teaching and preaching, and putting on paper the ideas that kept welling up in his fertile mind.

For Schweitzer wasn't going to China. He was going to a part of equatorial Africa that knew nothing of the amenities of civilization and build there, from the ground up, a place that could answer the medical needs of the local people. Soon after his arrival he was nearly overwhelmed by the sheer number of sick Africans coming out of the forest, suffering from an extraordinary variety of sicknesses—skin diseases, malaria, sleeping sickness, elephantiasis, heart problems, leprosy, osteomyelitis, dysentery, and hernia. The sick belonged to different tribes, spoke mutually incomprehensible languages, showed indifference and sometimes hostility toward one another.

Schweitzer was not only medical doctor but also foreman and laborer. He toiled and sweated under tropical heat for long hours every day, periodically suffered from dysentery, ulcers on his feet, sheer exhaustion, and, truth to tell, discouragement because of the unhelpfulness and incomprehension of his African patients. A man who rescued ants out of the postholes dug for the wooden piles, who worked in semidarkness at his desk for fear that a lit lantern might tempt moths to their death, was certainly a man of goodwill. A man who, even as a child, had a passion for equality certainly yearned to treat the Africans who came to him for treatment as his equals. "We are all brothers," he declared and then added realistically, "but I am the elder brother!"

Albert Schweitzer was elder brother to his three sisters and a younger brother. Outside the family, Schweitzer, by virtue of his imposing physical presence, talent, and intellectual achievements, was—even in his twenties—"elder brother" to the congregations of which he was the curate and to the students for whom he was the professor. At Lambaréné the European doctors and nurses who served with him also served under him. Schweitzer was "le docteur," and so when he required them to wear helmets as protection against sunstroke they obeyed, though some didn't think it necessary and complied only to humor the good doctor. When, however, Schweitzer required his African patients and their camp followers to wear sandals as a protection against foot disease, some obeyed, but many laughed it off, much to the doctor's chagrin and, yes, annoyance.

Was Schweitzer too committed to order and efficiency at his hospital? A German national of Lutheran upbringing might be expected to fit the stereotype, but Schweitzer didn't fit. To the contrary, some of his European and American visitors thought that his hospital compound was organized too much like an African village, with patients' families camping near their beds and goats and chickens running loose. Needless to say, a certain level of order and procedure had to be followed for the hospital to function at all. The Africans' lack of appreciation for hospital rules tried Schweitzer's patience. He used harsh words at times, only to apologize later.[54]

Schweitzer died peacefully at 11:30 p.m. on 4 September 1965 in the hospital he built. He was ninety years and eight months old. More than forty years of his life had been spent with the people of the equatorial forest. His long service there and his many intellectual and artistic accomplishments commanded great respect.

Honors followed one after another. In a two-year period (1953–55), for example, he was awarded the Nobel Peace Prize, Britain's Order of Merit, Germany's Order of Merit, and an honorary doctor of jurisprudence from Cambridge University. People in all walks of life, especially those in Europe and North America, admired him to the point of adulation. In more than one magazine survey they voted him "the greatest man in the world."

Even as honors poured in, so did criticisms. Many were ill informed, some were venomous. He was accused of being paternalistic and even racist, a publicity seeker and a medical incompetent who held up progress. The attacks gained surprisingly quick acceptance in some quarters, as though people were waiting in the wings to expose the feet of clay on a man they once felt obliged to admire. Deciding that Schweitzer was not a saint, they (mostly journalists and political commentators) concluded that he must be a fraud.

So who was Schweitzer? What manner of a man was he? Let me summarize some of his qualities. One is self-knowledge. A bad human being is often self-deceived, a good one rarely is. Schweitzer as a child was stung by a bee. Shrieking in terror and pain, he was instantly the center of attention, hugged and kissed, which he much liked. So he continued to cry long after the pain had disappeared. What made this child special was that he knew the temptation to use pretense and falsehood to attract attention and took care to be on guard against them. Whenever so tempted later in life, Schweitzer would tell himself to remember the bee.[55] Of the other defects he recognized in himself, one was a quick temper and a tendency to judge Africans unfairly when he was exhausted and irritable. Unrelenting demands of the hospital didn't give him much time to talk with Africans person to person rather than doctor to patient and so to appreciate the quality of their minds and not just the distressed state of their bodies. Yet, being self-aware, he could see this as an excuse; after all, in the evenings he was able to find time to write drafts of a book on civilization or play Bach on the antiquated piano. Schweitzer missed an opportunity to contribute to ethnography, for on the occasions he was able to talk leisurely with Africans, he found them eager to cogitate over the meaning of life and the nature of good and evil.[56]

Self-knowledge entails an awareness of one's blind spots. It is also to know that, no matter how hard one strives for integrity and harmoniousness, life is steeped in contradiction. Schweitzer tended not only sick people but also wounded animals that roamed the hospital compound. How did he do this? Well, among other things, he fed them other animals and fish. He felt guilt and was glad he felt it. "The good conscience," he said, "is an invention of the devil."[57]

Schweitzer had an appealing sense of humor, one that was laced with self-deprecation. In 1951, while he was traveling by train in America, two ladies approached his compartment and diffidently asked, "Have we the honor of speaking to Professor Einstein?" "No, unfortunately not," he replied. "However, he is a very old friend of mine—would you like me to give you his autograph?" And he wrote, "Albert Einstein, by way of his friend Albert Schweitzer." At Aspen, Colorado, reporters pestered Schweitzer with questions concerning his ideas about reverence for life, preventing him from eating his dinner. There was a distinction, Schweitzer finally said, between philosophy and practice. Now, as to practice, "if you let me go and eat my soup while it's warm, you've already practiced Reverence for Life." The reporters liked the retort and made it a part of the Schweitzer legend. Shortly after receiving the Nobel Peace Prize, Schweitzer was visited by a journalist who found the good doctor roaring at the dog chasing hens. "Stop that! Don't you know this is a Peace Prize house? Be a Nobel dog, and quick." Numerous visitors came to Lambaréné in the 1950s and 1960s. Many were shocked by the untidiness of the hospital compound. "Why, it's a zoo," cried one disenchanted guest. "Yes," Schweitzer said, "and I'm the chief gorilla."[58]

Self-knowledge and gentle humor do not define Schweitzer the man. What defines him is his sense of indebtedness, which was urgent and unrelenting. Where did it come from? Schweitzer's parents let him know that he was born a sickly infant and that there was doubt he would survive. Did he come to think of his life as a gift, a miracle? Perhaps. But other people have been told of their difficult birth without thereby feeling permanently thankful and indebted. Schweitzer gave his happy and privileged childhood and youth as the reason. Such happiness and privilege, he thought, put him under obligation to help others less fortunate. Yet was his childhood and youth really so privileged? The Schweitzer family was not well off. The five children were a strain on a pastor's salary. As for happiness, Schweitzer no doubt knew the occasional bursts of joy natural to the young and vigorous, but he had an introspective and moody temperament that militated against sustained contentment. He certainly won't do as a poster child of good behavior, for he had a streak of obstinacy that even slaps on the face from his irate father could not dent. Being both highly curious and critical, he engaged in interminable debates on theological points with adults at the dinner table, disregarding etiquette and the need to respect the views of his elders. One imagines that dinner at the family table could be rather tense.

Debt must be paid: an eye for an eye, a tooth for a tooth. Debt so conceived was totally alien to Schweitzer. The debts that weighed heavily on him were not the wrongs but "the rights" — health, talent, a supportive family, and the teachers who came his way. To him it was axiomatic that he couldn't just accept these smiles of fortune as his due. He must do something. He thought at first of starting an orphanage in Alsace. Heavy bureaucratic

red tape stood in his way. Then in 1904, through a chance encounter with an article in the Paris Evangelical Missionary Society
newsletter that called for workers in French equatorial Africa,
Schweitzer knew that his search was over. In that article he heard
Jesus's command "Follow me," and he could see that in following
the command he would be able to discharge a tiny portion of his
debt to a people who had been exploited, like so many others in
the world, so that he and his fellow Europeans could enjoy the
good life.

Gratitude is a recurrent theme in Schweitzer's thought and
life. He was grateful not just for the big gifts but also for the myriad small ones that crossed his path in the course of an ordinary
day. Here is an example: in 1918, the year the war ended, Schweitzer and his wife were released from a concentration camp and allowed to travel back to Alsace. They were both in poor health. "At
the station at Tarascon we had to wait in a distant shed for the arrival of our train. When it came, my wife and I, burdened with
heavy luggage, could hardly move. A poor cripple whom I had
treated in the camp came forward to help us. He had no baggage
because he had no possessions, and I was much moved by his
offer, which I accepted. While we walked side by side in the
scorching sun, I vowed to myself that in memory of him I would
in future always keep a lookout at stations for heavily laden people
and help them."[59]

The cripple discharged his debt to Schweitzer, and Schweitzer, touched, vowed to show his gratitude by helping others in similar need. And so the graces spread. "Discharging a debt" is not, however, quite the right expression, for it suggests legal obligation when the action may well be a natural and joyful response. Since gratitude is a pleasant feeling, one may be expected to welcome it. As a feeling, gratitude is, in fact, fairly common. Uncommon is making it public, expressing it to the person who helped. "Of the ten lepers whom Jesus healed, only one came back to him to thank him." That, Schweitzer felt, is not right. So to Scripture's admonition, "Never let the sun set on your anger," Schweitzer adds "and never postpone gratitude." We all need a little encouragement to do good, and since the effort required is minimal, why is gratitude so rarely given? The answer is not ingratitude but rather that we are easily distracted: we let the moment pass because, at that moment, the phone rings, the neighbor calls, or we inexplicably want to do the laundry.

"Do not be afraid to appear ridiculous" was another one of Schweitzer's favorite admonitions, one he had to give himself from time to time. Walking in a field with a child, he wanted to tell him not to pick flowers, for they would soon die in his hot little hand and he would discard them carelessly. But wasn't that advice, with its hint of reprimand, a little out of proportion to what, after all, would be a fairly innocent act? Walking down a poorly lit street, Schweitzer often felt an urge to help someone in need but refrained because the action could seem, even to himself, exaggerated. And what about failing to show gratitude? The ease with which we are distracted is not the only problem. We may also stifle a desire to express gratitude from fear of seeming needy, awkward, even obsequious.

Schweitzer was extremely frugal. He wore old clothes and old shoes, and in Europe he always traveled third-class. Frugality for Schweitzer was not an end in itself; it was yoked to his feeling for justice and equality. So in a sermon he urged: "Do not spend more on [beautiful and nice] things than you allow for the welfare of others! If you undertake a vacation trip, then set aside a gift that will go to the poor and sick to get them out of the muggy air. If you make a celebration for your relatives and friends, then ration your means so that you can offer the hungry the same amount you enjoyed to help them. If you buy a piece of furniture or something else that gives you pleasure, think about granting in the same value those who lack the most necessary things, who do not know how they are going to pay their rent."[60]

Schweitzer was a practical mystic. He used his sharp intellect to demythologize Jesus, pointing out that the man from Nazareth was human enough to be deluded by the imminent end of time, but this did not prevent Schweitzer from submitting unconditionally to Jesus's command of love. So, for Schweitzer, who is

Jesus? At the end of *The Quest of the Historical Jesus* he gives his answer. It is not to be found in labors of the mind but rather in action. "To those who obey him, be they wise or simple, he will reveal himself in the toils, the conflicts, the sufferings through which they shall pass in his company. As an ineffable mystery, they shall learn in their own experience who he is."[61]

The mystical streak in Schweitzer also appeared in his love of music. Music to him was as much a spiritual as an intellectual-aesthetic vocation. Immersing himself in Bach was, as he himself put it, "exactly the same as doing theology." The child Schweitzer's strong moral sense demanded an answer well above the conventional plane to a plane that can only be called religious. The child's sensitivity to music was similarly acute and deep. Taken to a concert at age eleven, he didn't understand how the audience could applaud enthusiastically and yet, after a while, lapse into silence to study the next item on the program, chat, and offer each other bonbons when he remained in a state of rapture.[62] Schweitzer's response to Jesus is, ultimately, a mystery. A man he met through the mildewed pages of history gave him such strength and confidence that his wearisome works of mercy could seem almost easy for lack of inner struggle or a sense of self-sacrifice. Music was also such a source of strength and consolation. Bach made him, and not him alone, see that one could take enormous delight in life and yet yearn for death.[63]

Simone Weil (1909–1943)

Confucius and Socrates were figures of some importance in their time, even though Confucius never attained the office he hoped for and Socrates was condemned to death for his impiety. Mozart was acclaimed in his lifetime. Keats, although he never enjoyed the acclaim Mozart had, was recognized as a poet of distinction and promise in the literary and artistic circles in which he moved. Schweitzer, as we have just seen, was famous in every sense of the word. Sharply different in fate from all these people was Simone Weil. She died relatively unknown at age thirty-four, the chief reason for her anonymity being that she published only a few papers in obscure journals in her lifetime. Her fame is posthumous; moreover, unlike that of Mozart and Schweitzer, it is largely limited to thinkers and scholars. Among them, in the sixty-odd years since her death, she is seen (in T. S. Eliot's words) as "a woman of genius, of a kind of genius akin to that of saints."[64] She also has detractors who, while they recognize the power of her mind, regard her thought as too one-sided and extreme and her own person as repressed, masochistically inclined to immolate herself in the name of love, justice, and a desire for perfection. She was both highly intellectual and grounded in the exact particulars of existence, both egoistical in the sense of wanting to retain her purity above all else and utterly selfless, both touchingly lovable and forbiddingly harsh. In short, she has the contradictions of all human beings, but these appear larger than life size in a saint; and saints, as George Orwell said, should always be held guilty until their innocence has been proved.

It is difficult to think of Albert Schweitzer and Simone Weil as contemporaries, yet they were. One reason for the difficulty is the contrast in life span: when Weil was born in 1909 Schweitzer was already attending the Third Congress of the International Music Society in Vienna as an authority on the organ; and when Weil died in 1943 Schweitzer had another twenty-two more years to live. A further difficulty in coupling these two persons in thought is that although both are much admired for their goodness, their personalities can hardly be more different: they followed opposite paths to virtue, Schweitzer's being affirmative, Weil's being negative. I have characterized Schweitzer as eminently sane, words that few people would want to apply to Weil. Without doubt, compared with Weil, Schweitzer is a much easier figure to understand, accept, and admire.

An advantage of studying one's contemporaries is that details of their childhood are more likely to be available. We know almost nothing about the childhoods of Confucius and Socrates, a bit more about those of Mozart and Keats, and much more about those of Schweitzer and Weil. Knowing more enables us to see when the traits that define an adult first appeared in life. In what ways were the child Schweitzer and the child Weil alike, and in what ways did they differ?

As we have seen, the boy Schweitzer didn't like to be privileged, to have things that other children didn't have. Weil likewise. Astonishingly, when she, barely three years old, was given a large sparkling ring, she declared, "I do not like luxury!" At age five she had already mastered the art of the put-down. Introduced to a very elegant and rather snobbish lady, she said, "Oh, you, you're the lady's maid." She did not like to dress too well and asserted that "it would be better if everyone was dressed in the same way and for a sou. That way people could work and no differences would be apparent among them." Her passion for social justice was irrepressible and urgent. It wasn't just a subjective feeling. She diligently sought to know how injustice came about and what were its remedies. At age eleven, for example, she attended meetings of the unemployed.[65] How many young girls of her social class would want to do that? The boy Schweitzer argued strenuously for his views with his father. Weil showed similar confidence and stubbornness. Even as a six year old she would present her ideas with such aplomb that her parents, at first annoyed, ended laughing. Schweitzer and Weil as children differed in their intellectual interests. Through his midteens Schweitzer was mostly concerned with philosophical and theological issues that were the dinner-table talk of his family. By contrast, literature and mathematics engaged

Weil's attention. At a tender age Simone and her older brother André challenged each other to recite long passages of Corneille and Racine, and whoever made a mistake got a slap from the other.[66] It was a game for the precocious and fun-loving siblings, but, for Simone, literature was also taken with extreme seriousness because it raised for her questions of good and evil—of morality. As for mathematics, Simone caught fire from André, who first revealed his extraordinary talent at age nine. He found an older cousin's textbook on mathematics, read it as one might a novel, and solved the equations in it on his own. Both children loved mathematics, at first no doubt as a mind-teasing game, then for its beauty, and finally, for Simone, as the language of truth, a hint of the divine.

Young Schweitzer felt compassion for animals. Throughout his life, nature meant for him primarily living creatures. By contrast, young Simone was ecstatic about sunsets. Whenever she heard that she could see a sunset, she would drop everything to run and see it. At age sixteen, when she and her family went to the Alps for their holiday, Simone saw ice fields in the midst of towering mountains for the first time. These sublime features of the earth inspired in her an idea of purity that remained with her for the rest of her life. At the other end of nature's scale were flowers and butterflies. Four-year-old Simone and seven-year-old André, during a Swiss holiday, picked flowers and caught butterflies, which they would immediately free, for both were full of pity for living things. Schweitzer's reverence for life extended even to snowflakes and spring water, but, perhaps because in childhood he never left the thoroughly humanized landscapes of Alsace, he never developed a religious or even romantic appreciation for wildness—for nature on a stupendous scale. The exception might be the tropical forest that eventually became his home. Schweitzer, however, respected rather than admired the tropical forest. Given its mixture of growth and decay, its harboring of life and disease, he could hardly see it as an unadulterated image of beauty and purity.

A criticism of Schweitzer's ethics is that he was too little engaged with questions of social justice, although it was in the name of justice and restitution that the good doctor spent more than half of his long life alleviating pain among African peoples. A criticism of Weil's ethics is that she has very little to say about animals, and this lacuna occurs despite her keen interest in the oppressed and humiliated, which animals—especially domesticated animals—certainly were and are. Puzzling, too, is how she could be such an admirer of Saint Francis and not dwell on that saint's tenderness toward all God's creatures. When she did make a comment, her thought was characteristically trenchant and to the point. In one of her notebooks she jotted down the words: "One must either not eat any meat, not kill any animals; or look upon animals as machines after the style of Descartes; or surround their death with certain religious images." And here she added the example of a tribe of cattle herders in Africa who imagined that animals allowed themselves to be killed to feed human beings. Unless we face up to these positions, "what is more calculated," she asked, "to take away all notion of morality from children?"[67]

In regard to human beings Weil was an extreme egalitarian. She was an egalitarian in the traditionally understood sense of wanting change toward a more even distribution of power and wealth. She fought for the oppressed, and she did so with every fiber of her being and with all the means, including force, at her disposal. She was called a Communist and, more cuttingly, the "Red virgin," even though she was never a party member. As a university student and, later, a philosophy teacher at various schools in the 1920s and 1930s, Weil's leftist leaning hardly made her stand out among her peers. What did make her stand out and apart was her eventual conclusion—a jeer at Marx—that revolution, not religion, is the opiate of the people.[68]

Revolution, even if it could be achieved without bloodshed, merely reversed status, like turning over an hourglass. The idea that a worker, after an immense struggle, could one day live like a bourgeois, strutting down the Champs-Élysées swinging a cane, would be funny if it were not so delusory and sad. For Weil, such a change in the human condition represented a fall, not an improvement. As for a future world of social justice in which each and every person can fulfill his or her potential, that, to Weil, was pure daydreaming. Weil wanted, of course, social justice. She fought for adequate material compensation, but more than anything else she wanted factories to be so run that workers could see and understand the ends of their labor. Should this happen, they would be exercising both mind and muscles. To Weil such a life would be superior to the life of people like herself who only used their minds and who, for lack of direct contact with matter, were especially prone to fantasy.

Achieving a degree of equality for all social groups was not, in the end, the real problem for Weil. Conceivably, under the right conditions, it can be done, as it is more or less done in a mature democracy such as Sweden. The real problem, for Weil, was locating the grounds for equality among individuals, for in every respect one can think of—beauty, strength, talent, temperament, condition of upbringing, and so on—individuals are strikingly unequal. Some are favored, others are not or are less so. Does it matter? Not really, says Weil, for to her that which really matters is access to truth—to reality. She explained how she arrived at her position in a story she told about herself:

> At the age of fourteen I fell into one of those fits of bottomless despair which come with adolescence; and I seriously thought of dying, because of the mediocrity of my natural faculties. The extraordinary gifts of my brother, who had a childhood and youth comparable to those of Pascal, made me forcibly aware of

this. What I minded was not the lack of external successes but the having no hope of access to that transcendent realm where only the truly great can enter and where truth dwells. I felt it better to die than to live without truth.

After months of inner darkness I gained, suddenly and for ever, the certainty that any human being at all, even if his natural faculties are almost nil, can find his way into the realm of truth which is reserved for genius, if only he longs for truth and makes a perpetual effort of attention so as to reach it. In this way he too becomes a genius, even though, for want of talent, no genius is externally visible.[69]

Any human being can have access to truth. The problem for Weil was not the desire per se, for she saw it embedded at the center of every person. The problem was the "what" that is desired. The "what" for all animals are food, water, shelter, and sexual satisfaction. For human beings, to these basics are added such extras as personal distinction in talent and beauty, wealth, prestige, and power. Although everyone may have these desires, their attainment in life—the amount apportioned to each person by fate—differs enormously, and so we see in the world the extreme inequalities of prince and pauper, palace and hovel, exceptional talent and no talent, startling beauty and repellent ugliness. But Weil will say, What does it matter, if, untalented and poor, one can still hope to catch, through the purity of one's desire, glimpses of truth, beauty, and justice in the transcendental realm—or God?

Truth, beauty, and justice. The usual presumption is that access to these supreme goods also requires one to be well-to-do and well educated: thus, truth is for the scholar and scientist, beauty is for the artist and aesthetician, and justice is for the well connected. If so, one must conclude that truth, beauty, and justice—insofar as they are embodied in works of art and science and in courts of law—are likewise beyond the reach of the underprivileged. This lack of access would certainly constitute a deprivation, but it can be removed by changing society, which is not impossible. But what if the handicap is a deficiency in talent caused not by society but by nature? Remember that Weil considered herself lacking the talent necessary to enter the realm of transcendent truth. Her answer to this personal and individual injustice lay in drawing a sharp distinction between talent and genius. Talent, as she saw it, can never carry one very far because it is detached from morality; talent is not buoyed by that desire for perfect beauty, perfect truth, and perfect justice that are at the core of morality. Talent may bring power and success, but, in the end, it has no greatness. It is genius that has greatness, genius that gives us works of beauty, truth, and justice—three virtues that, though separable in concept, are nearly indistinguishable in experience.[70]

To the nonphilosopher, statements of this kind can sound hopelessly abstract. Weil, never one to hide behind abstractions, boldly offers particular works to make her point. "In Giotto," she maintains, "it is not possible to distinguish between the genius of the painter and the Franciscan spirit [that is, Franciscan morality]; nor in the pictures and poems produced by the Zen sect in China between the painter's or poet's genius and the state of mystical illumination [or transcendent goodness]." And then Weil says, outrageously to some, luminously to others: "From the purely poetic point of view, without taking into account anything else, it is infinitely preferable to have written the Canticle of St. Francis of Assisi, that jewel of perfect beauty, than the entire works of Victor Hugo."[71]

To every human being who wants to be touched by the triune of truth, beauty, and justice (God), all that is required is pure desire and a willingness to wait, which, to Weil, amounts to praying. Ask for bread, and one may or may not receive it, but ask for *spiritual* bread (the word "spiritual," Weil notes, is in Jerome's translation of the Lord's Prayer), and the granting is certain. Spiritual bread is God and his work—the universe and works of human genius. Any person, even if he or she is not very bright, can still rejoice in such natural things as a glorious sunset, a night sky filled with stars, and a warm smile. Works of human talent, which is to say, the bulk of literature, art, and music in the world, are probably outside such a person's ken. Should this be considered an insufferable deprivation? No, says Weil, for she believes that even if works of talent are inaccessible to the ungifted, works of genius are accessible to everyone. And among such works Weil includes (besides the ones mentioned above) Euclidean geometry and Greek science, Homer's *Iliad,* the plays of Aeschylus and Sophocles, Shakespeare's *King Lear,* Racine's *Phèdre,* the poems of Villon, Gregorian chant, and the music of Bach, Mozart, and Monteverdi. They are, of course, very different. What do they have in common? They have in common, Weil would have said, balance and harmony, a natural feel for limit or completion, as in a circle or, to put it more grandly, as in the Circle of Perfection, a Pythagorean idea that, in the seventeenth century, was called "one of the most convenient Hieroglyphicks of God."[72]

A more obvious reason why a work of genius is more easily appreciated is that it tends to be simpler and more lucid. A poem by Saint Francis is simpler and more lucid than the collected works of Victor Hugo, Gregorian chant than Wagner's *Ring,* the andante of Bach's Brandenburg Concerto no. 4 than Mahler's Symphony no. 2, the "Resurrection." Given the right kind of guidance and under the right conditions, I should be able to intuit the goodness and truth of a Bach cantata, even if understanding it in a technical and analytical way is beyond me. This is a loss, but not a great loss when one considers that a listener too technically engaged in the construction of a musical composition might be disabled from responding to it as a full human being, endowed with mind and heart.

Weil also believed that the oppressed and handicapped have access to mathematics and science in the sense that they can have a notion of the truth, beauty, and justice of mathematics and science even if the technical steps in reasoning are beyond them. It might seem strange to use the exalted words truth, beauty, and justice in regard to school subjects that are commonly seen as dull, yet mathematicians and scientists habitually say that they aspire to beauty, and, of course, they pursue truth. Furthermore, from the way they employ concepts such as equilibrium and balance, they may also be said to thirst for justice. Based on her experience teaching factory and farm workers, Weil concluded that anyone at all, provided he or she has that combination of desire and attentiveness, is able to appreciate the basic principles of science. And that, to Weil, is like saying that one can touch the hem of God.

Weil felt a natural affinity for the poor and the heavily laden. She was at ease and at home in their midst. Weil also thought that the poor and the heavily laden enjoyed a special privilege—the privilege of direct contact with reality. In her view, the well-to-do, protected from physical labor and the harassments of nature and society, are not quite real. Their whole way of life makes for easy escapism. The poor and heavily laden cannot so easily escape.

Harsh reality too often intrudes and binds them to earth. "When an apprentice gets hurt, or complains of being tired," Weil says, "the workmen and peasants have this fine expression: 'It is the trade entering his body.'" The lesson she draws from this remark is: "Each time that we have some pain to go through, we can say to ourselves quite truly that it is the universe, the order, and beauty of the world and the obedience of creation to God that are entering our body."[73]

The "we" that Weil uses here is "everyone." Everyone knows pain. But no doubt she had in mind, above all, those who work with their body. "Pain unites humans and animals," Albert Schweitzer might say. "It is something they all know." And pain is to be relieved whenever and wherever possible. That's the ideal of the affirmative way. The negative way requires that one accept pain—an idea that, in the pampered society of our day, immediately raises the red flag of perversion and masochism. Yet we all know from experience that pain is often welcomed. When offered the choice between enjoying a photo of our beloved and being hugged by him or her to the point of pain, there can be no doubt as to where the choice lies. A more common example is this: the gardener indisputably enjoys the ache in her body and may well feel somewhat deprived—that she has not done enough—until the ache reaches a certain level. For pain, understood in a certain way, *is* to be penetrated by the world, gripped by the world, hugged by the world, loved by the world, and, since the world—the totality of things—is created by God, loved by God.

Simone Weil worked for a year in a factory and for varying lengths of time on the land. She wanted to feel her world shrinking to the confines of her body under the relentless pressure of pain and fatigue. Anyone keen to learn realistic methods of improving the condition of work in an industrial society needed, she believed, such direct experience and knowledge. Her dedication to the task was heroic: besides the work experience itself, she studied the large literature on socioeconomic reform, from ephemeral essays to the weighty tomes of Karl Marx, joined and led trade union movements, badgered owners of factories and farms, spoke at public meetings, participated in marches, distributed pamphlets, wrote and published articles. While she was doing all this she was also earning her living as a lycée professor. She so exhausted herself that, from time to time, she had to take sick leave.

Teaching being Weil's profession, it naturally occurred to her that even if the system that oppressed workers could not be changed anytime soon, it should be possible to start improving their condition by giving them the sort of knowledge that makes their work meaningful. The knowledge has to be relevant. So much of what workers learn in school is irrelevant to their occupation. Her friendship with workers—especially the young—convinced her that there exists a correlation between their intelligence and goodness and a genuine interest in general concepts. The interest is all the greater if the concepts can throw light on the work they do. In her ideal program of studies, machine work would be backed by the science of mechanics, metal work by metallurgy and materials science, farm work by astronomy and geography—the movement of the stars, the cycle of seasons, the causes of rain and drought, the nature of light and heat.

At every opportunity Weil gave free lessons to her fellow workers. Well-educated friends considered these ventures quixotic. True, the older workers and peasants may have felt confused, embarrassed, and bored, but the younger ones were known to have come under her spell, for Weil, with her deep knowledge, skillful exposition, and a real interest in the individual student, could be irresistible.

One touching example is this letter, dated 1932, that a young carpenter wrote to Weil, who taught him geometry. "In the three lessons I had with you, you have given me all the elementary facts of geometry; it is a pity that I cannot see you more often, for I would have ended by becoming a truly learned person. What was really marvelous about it is that I remember almost everything you taught me . . . and that with you as the teacher I was never bored for a second; and these few instants exalt all the noble thoughts that inhabits me. If I could see you more often, I would make double progress, intellectual as well as moral."[74] Let me underline this important point: the young man felt that noble thoughts inhabited him and that he had made both intellectual and moral progress. Without doubt, this progress in mind and morals, far more than mere higher wages, was the kind of liberation Weil wished for all workers.

Science is rooted in religion and morality. Although the ancient Greeks knew and accepted the intimate relatedness, we moderns have come to be deeply suspicious and strive to keep science, religion, and morality firmly apart. We do so for the good reason that, historically, religion and morality have too often interfered with science. Simone Weil believed, however, that the rigid disconnection also entails a loss—the loss of a coherent worldview. The severance, to her, is unnatural. Moreover, even now it is not total. A hint of their intimate bond remains. Weil makes us see it by her use of the words "force," "necessity," and "obedience."

"Force" is the operative word in science. It pervades the universe, and the universe—let us remind ourselves—includes human society, human biology, and human psychology. For all our vaunted freedom, we humans are subject to force, pushed this way and that; or, if we are at a standstill, it means only that we are at a point where the forces happen to balance. Force at the impersonal level of science is necessity at the level of felt experience. We live under necessity—sleep under biological necessity, brush our teeth under biosocial necessity, take our hat off to the boss under social necessity. Force at the impersonal level and necessity at the personal level are obedience at the level of morality and religion—obedience, ultimately, to God, the source of all force and the laws that govern it.[75]

Whereas human beings can assert a will seemingly their own and so choose to be disobedient, matter is entirely passive and in consequence entirely obedient to God's will. The result of such passivity and obedience is, in Weil's words, "the beauty of the world." In the beauty of the world brute force and necessity become an object of love. "What is more beautiful than the action of gravity on the fugitive folds of the sea waves, or on the almost eternal folds of the mountains?" She continues: "The sea is not less beautiful in our eyes because we know that sometimes ships are wrecked by it. On the contrary, this adds to its beauty. If it altered the movement of its waves to spare a boat, it would be a creature gifted with discernment and choice and not this fluid, perfectly obedient to every external pressure. It is this perfect obedience that constitutes the sea's beauty."[76]

Simone Weil died in a sanatorium in Ashford, England. The medical officer judged her death to be by starvation "while the balance of her mind was disturbed." Even in a state of extreme weakness she refused to eat more than her starving compatriots in France. This was not at all unusual for her. All her life, even as a child, she wanted to give away what she had so as to establish some sort of equality with the people among whom she lived. Money that she earned flowed from her to needy students, fellow workers, acquaintances, and strangers as water flowed downhill— that is, as though in obedience to a law of nature. This being so, she never felt her action to be charity or even generosity. Weil knew perfectly well that giving could also be a power play, and she made sure that the recipient of her largesse never felt in any sense diminished. She gave not only her material goods but also her energy and time—babysitting for a working mother, coaching her landlady's son in his schoolwork, taking care of a beggar neglected in the hospital, writing encouraging letters to inmates in concentration camps, and so on. Again, she did all these things not from duty, the exercising of an indomitable and righteous will, but naturally. Nevertheless, such relentless emptying of self must sooner or later lead to total exhaustion; more than once it led her to the threshold of death and on 24 August 1943, at 10:30 p.m., to death itself.

If this be goodness, it is inhuman goodness. To someone like George Orwell, Weil stands guilty of sainthood. But was she even "good" in an ordinary human sense? For she could be cutting, thoughtless, and aloof—"an intellectual monster," as someone put it. There are reasons, however, for these lapses of civility and consideration. For one, she never learned the art of small talk, of making pleasantries to avoid disagreement and confrontation. For another, her conversation, rich in historical references and forceful argumentation, could make her seem cold and aloof to the less intellectually inclined. A third trait that made her stand out was her habit of giving the view opposed to hers equal hearing—a consequence of her passion for truth and justice. A fourth was her lack of a self-protective ego: like a child, she said things she believed in without the least heed as to whether they might earn her scorn. And so, yes, she could be direct and bold to the point of rudeness, but only in the company of her self-assured peers. To those who did not have her social and educational advantages—and her friends included many such—she was the soul of patience and gentleness.

Even as a little girl of five Simone Weil showed her toughness, her stoicism. Shivering in the cold water of her bathtub, she declaimed the famous words of Turenne, general to Louis XIV (uttered on the battlefield, when he was in danger): "You tremble, carcass."[77] Her mother, who was by her side, must have been astonished! At a very early age Weil already appeared to have chosen the negative way. She recognized, however, the equal validity of the way of affirmation and even had a talent for it. When not laid low by fatigue and a headache, her delight in the wonderful creations of God and man was almost Franciscan. Letters written from Italy in 1937 contain many instances of rapturous appreciation. About Ferrara and Ravenna she wrote: "Two really beautiful towns. . . . At Ravenna—it was market day—humanity was beautiful too, especially the young peasants. When Providence places beautiful people among beautiful things, it is a superabundance of grace. Every day, in this country, one notes in certain men of the people a nobility and a simplicity of manner and attitude that compel admiration." She loved Florence and its surrounding landscape. "Oh, but Florence is beautiful from high up there, with the sun setting! . . . The Viale dei Colli is full of aromatic odors that go to your head, above all with the view of those slopes covered with olive trees." But it was at Assisi that she grew truly ecstatic. "At Assisi I forgot all about Milan, Florence, Rome, and the rest; I was so overcome by such graceful landscapes, so miraculously evangelical and Franciscan, . . . and those noble examples of the human race, the Umbrian peasants—so well favored, so healthy, so vigorous and happy and gentle."[78]

Simone Weil was accused of being sexually repressed. It is more true to say that she deliberately sublimated her physical needs and urges so that she could partake of spiritual bread—spiritual in the sense Saint Jerome meant it. As one might expect, she had read Freud and was unimpressed; she much preferred Plato's erotic psychology. Far from being a prude, young Simone openly admired the charms of the opposite sex. She might even flirt. In the train to Assisi she fraternized with young workmen back from Abyssinia. "One of them, who spoke French, told me that he would soon be going to Paris. I gave him my address. The result:

an hour later he proposed that we get married when he comes to France. I told him that I had not known him long enough." After her first journey to Italy she said to Simone Pétrement, her closest friend at the École Normale Supérieure, with a smile, "I went there to see if I could meet Tommasco Cavalieri, but I never did meet him." (Tommasco Cavalieri was the young and handsome nobleman to whom Michelangelo addressed some of his love poems.) To another friend she wrote: "Ever since I've been in Florence, I've been looking around to see if I can recognize Tommasco Cavalieri, but I haven't seen him yet. Perhaps it is just as well, because if I did meet him, I should have to be dragged away from Florence by main force." Of course, she was joking, but it was not just a joke. She found happiness and uplift in beautiful and good human beings. There again, she showed herself to be a disciple of Plato.[79]

Simone Weil was inspired by ancient Greek thinkers. She was also inspired by the Gospels, the figure of Jesus, and the rituals of the Catholic Church. She felt that she had a naturally Christian soul, that she was born a Christian. Her awareness of the close bond came, however, by slow stages in large part because, as she liked to say, she never sought God. The first explicit awareness came in 1935, while she was on vacation in Portugal. She was alone one evening and found herself walking by a very poor fishing village. It happened to be the feast day of its patron saint, and the women, carrying candles, were visiting all the ships in procession and chanting a hymn of great sadness. "There, the certainty suddenly came to me that Christianity is pre-eminently the religion of slaves, that slaves cannot help adhering to it, and I among the others." The second occasion when she felt compelled to acknowledge something she still resisted was in 1937. She was again alone, this time in the chapel of Santa Maria degli Angeli, where Saint Francis had often prayed. She herself did not intend to pray, yet she knelt down as though impelled "by something stronger than myself."[80] The third occasion was in 1938. An unrelenting headache forced Weil to take a leave from teaching. With the headache still intense, she went with her mother to Solesmes in northwestern France to hear the Gregorian chant at Easter services. There she made a supreme effort of attention. As she described it later, the effort of attention "enabled me to get outside this miserable flesh, leaving it to suffer by itself, heaped up in its corner, and to find a pure and perfect joy in the unspeakable beauty of chanting and the words. This experience enabled me by analogy to understand better the possibility of loving the divine love in the midst of affliction."

At Solesmes she met a young Englishman who introduced her to the seventeenth-century English metaphysical poets, in particular, George Herbert. She sat down to read Herbert's poems. Her splitting headache notwithstanding, she read them with her characteristic total attention. One poem stopped her in her tracks by its beauty—its conveyance of the divine through homespun images. The poem is called "Love."

> Love bade me welcome; yet my soul drew back,
> Guiltie of dust and sinne,
> But quick-ey'd Love, observing me grow slack
> From my first entrance in,
> Drew nearer to me, sweetly questioning
> If I lack'd any thing.
>
> A guest, I answer'd, worthy to be here:
> Love said, You shall be he.
> I the unkinde, ungrateful? Ah my deare,
> I cannot look on thee.
> Love took my hand, and smiling did reply,
> Who made the eyes but I?
>
> Truth Lord, but I have marr'd them; let my shame
> Go where it doth deserve.
> And know you not, sayest Love, who bore the blame?
> My dear, then I will serve.
> You must sit down, sayest Love, and taste my meat:
> So I did sit and eat.[81]

Simone Weil memorized the poem, thinking at first that she liked it for its aesthetic qualities, but she soon realized that it had become for her a form of prayer. Four years after this experience she recounted it to Father Perrin, a Dominican monk, and said as she recited the poem, "Christ himself came down and took possession of me."[82]

Weil, despite her natural bent toward Christianity and despite the experiences related above, resisted baptism. She did so for a variety of reasons. Two stood out. First, although she liked the church's sacraments and solemn rituals, she didn't at all care for its institutional pomp and wealth. She once said, "If only there were a notice on church doors forbidding entry to anyone with an income above a certain figure, and that a low one, I would be converted at once."[83] The church, she thought, was unable to free itself from the taint of worldliness that it had acquired through its close association with imperial Rome. The second major reason is that, for her, the Catholic Church was not nearly catholic—that is, universal—enough: it excluded, through the hated word "anathema," so much that she loved in other religious traditions and philosophies. To use her intellect to the full in the service of Christ as the Truth, she felt compelled to put herself at a certain distance from the institution, for, in her exchanges with priests, she could see that their views had been slanted by their patriotism toward the church as an earthly country. So Weil waited outside—just outside—for God himself to give her the final shove. That shove apparently never came.

A test of sainthood is whether the person was widely and deeply loved. That seems to me even more convincing than an enumeration of good deeds, which can all be performed for mixed motives. Simone Weil was deeply loved by her family, her students, intellectuals and artists, factory workers and farmhands, her fellow countrymen and aliens, men and women, old and young. They loved her for her courage and selflessness, generosity and gaiety, imagination and learning, charm and purity, and, yes, even for such shortcomings as her manual awkwardness, her untidiness, and her only self-indulgence—chain smoking. And so it is possible to admire her to the point of veneration and yet feel protective toward her as one would toward a younger sister or be irritated by her to the point of total exasperation and yet feel the sort of fondness one has for a headstrong younger brother. But perhaps the most convincing test of whether a person is truly good—a saint—is this. In his or her presence, does one feel oneself a better and more intelligent human being? By all accounts, Simone Weil passed that test.

4

Reflections

At the beginning of this book I referred to Stephen Jay Gould's expression the "ten thousand acts of kindness" that illuminate the human stage every day, making it—on the whole—a good place for people. I also said that, given the amount of evil on almost every page of world history, one can't help wondering whether these ten thousand acts of kindness are only points of light in a night sky of unrelenting darkness. Further illustrating this rather bleak view is the famous opening line of the Gospel according to John, "The light shines in darkness, and the darkness overcomes it not," which makes one wonder whether light can do more than just hold its ground, whether it can expand into the dark realm, diminishing if not conquering it.

Another thesis I raised is that, in real life, good people and virtuous acts are enduringly captivating and rewarding, whereas bad people and malevolent acts are boring, even if they give a momentary thrill at first encounter. Now this can only be true—this is even obviously true—if somehow we see human goodness as points of light against a gray or black backdrop. After all, looking up at the night sky, the stars rather than the darkness catch our attention.

But these are metaphors. In down-to-earth language I am saying that good people and good acts stand out against a gray background of biosocial behavior and against a darker background of evil. These backgrounds, both gray and black, lend themselves to quasi-scientific study because the events in them exhibit the repetitiousness—the patterned occurrences and recurrences—of nature. Social scientists study the backgrounds. Storytellers are drawn to the exceptions. However, they appear to be more drawn to exceptional evil than to exceptional good, and in this respect they are no different from newspaper publishers and their readers. I seek to rectify the bias by urging my fellow humans to do what comes naturally to us, namely, pay attention to the exceptional but with the understanding that genuine goodness is the truly exceptional. It, rather than biosocial or evil behavior, challenges easy scientific accounting.

Dark Background

Here are a few basic facts about our nature that go some way to explaining why evil so often blights our lives. First is the undeniable fact of our destructiveness. We destroy for the sense of power it gives us. An infant too uncoordinated to raise a wood-block tower destroys it gleefully with a swipe of his or her arm. A toddler too young to set the table pulls the tablecloth and happily sends the plates crushing to the floor. These acts of violence are our first accomplishments, tokens of our power to make a difference. And, if we are honest, we will admit that in adulthood we retain a certain fascination for the car crash, the steel ball smashing into a derelict building, and even for the theater of violence (the battlefield), provided we are at a safe distance.

When we destroy wantonly, as we often do, we reveal a dark side of our nature. But we not only destroy wantonly; we also *have* to destroy if only to build: we kill and eat to build our bodies, cut down trees to build our houses, clear an entire forest to build a village, town, and adjoining farms, and so on. Is any of life's myriad activities exempt from some kind of destructiveness and violence? Even the sex act—and what act is more constructive than that?—can be violent to a degree unknown in the animal world. Those who try to civilize it, remove from it the entanglement and writhing of sweaty limbs, will end by making it humdrum, hardly worth the effort of undressing. Moreover, let's admit that we enjoy the frenzy in sexual conjugation, enjoy even the domination and submission that it momentarily entails. Sexual passion, however, easily gets out of hand such that violence wholly takes over; pleasure becomes asymmetrical in that it resides only in the strong and lies more in the sheer exercising of power over another than in erotic charge, although the latter never quite disappears.

Sex is play, and being able to play with another—treat him or her as our whim dictates—is an intoxicating actualization of power. We all engage in it if only in the fairly harmless social game of manipulating someone so that he or she, perhaps unknowingly, does what we want. Playing loses all innocence, it becomes evil when, in a lopsided relationship of power, we act upon another against his or her will. This happens more often than we are willing to admit in the family and, indeed, in any hierarchically organized institution. Playing with another is not only egregious but carries no shame when plants and animals are the other. We train and breed them so that they conform to our fantasy. Dwarfing trees so that they fit into a smallish porcelain bowl, dwarfing canines so that they can sit and warm our laps are some well-known instances of extreme domination, yet they are carried out in a spirit of playfulness.[1]

Violence, even intraspecific killing, is a fairly common occurrence in the animal world. Humans, surprisingly, do not slaughter their own kind. True, we kill other people on a massive scale in war and in genocide, but only because we do not see them as fully human. To the ancient Greeks, non-Greeks were barbarians, and the word "barbarian" was an imitation of the animal sounds that foreigners supposedly made. This is a much quoted example, and I could easily have picked some other. The fact is, few exceptions exist to the rule that only "we" (the insiders) are fully human and "they" (the outsiders) are not, or not quite.[2] Hence, if circumstances demand or opportunities arise, "they" can be enslaved, domesticated, or killed as animals are. If we are shocked, it is because we so easily forget our propensity for violence, even though reminders are all around us. Think of the stockyard and the slaughterhouse, bad odors from food-processing plants and tanning factories, mounted animal heads in a hunter's lodge, leather goods and furs in fancy stores. True, we do not run into these reminders every day. But in the home itself evidences of violence are hardly hidden; it is just that we do not register what we see, blinded by habituation. And what telltale signs do we find lying about our homes? In the basement are rat poison and weed killer, on the blood-stained cutting board is the kitchen knife, on the dining table is a succulent roast, and even as newspaper headlines and television screens announce mayhem in the next neighborhood, the host politely enquires, "breast or leg?" as a dismembered turkey is passed around.

A large brain empowers us to imagine, fantasize, and think in ways that far exceed those of other animals. They have given our species the upper hand in evolutionary domination. But they also carry a disadvantage, which, ironically, is just this awareness.

Awareness of a uniquely human kind directs us not only to the external world but also to the self, making us realize against our will that we will die and rot, and so we feel a vulnerability that no other animals feel. Another unwelcome discovery is emptiness—a void—that lies at the core of our being. Any time we are alone, unoccupied with a task, we are confronted by this void, which itself is a reminder of death. Hence we seek to be with our kind, not only for collective strength, as animals do, but also for anonymity and to englut emptiness. We need to belong, which means that we must be willing to conform, and, as a matter of fact, we are pathetically willing to conform, for good but also for great evil.

Another way to englut emptiness and put off the thought of death is to identify our self with what we have. The more we have, the more we *are*. With a thousand pairs of shoes in the closet, how can I, or anyone else, doubt my existence—my enduring existence? Human greed for possession is insatiable because no matter how many things I have, they can never quite dull the aching void at the core of my being. Nevertheless, possession remains a real temptation. At least temporarily, it keeps inflated my collapsing sense of self, and, moreover, it can provide me with an illusion of power.

Power as such, and especially power over other people, can make me feel strong and immortal, godlike. Having people constantly at my beck and call is intoxicating, all the more so if my power is such that whether another lives or dies depends on my whim. Death itself, then, could seem my servant; and a servant who consistently obeys my command will not and cannot turn against me.

That bullies find their way into the family, school, corporation, and government ought not to surprise us: bending another's will to conform with one's own is a perverse but real source of satisfaction. Nor is the ubiquity of greed surprising: if Mrs. Marcos has far more shoes than she can wear, I have far more books than I can read. Since neither power nor possession enduringly fulfills, and since what I have always can seem less than what others have, envy subtly poisons my relation with others. Envy is uniquely humbling, for it implies a deep lack in me that is intolerable to admit. I therefore turn away from myself to belittle others, cut them down to my size so that they too can feel like ciphers. Belittling the other in small and large ways, day in and day out, is a mark of our intelligence. No other animal does it. Envy may seem a small evil, but it builds up. And because it builds up under a brittle carapace of pretend goodwill, it can erupt—when circumstances are right—into murderous hatred.

Besides power and wealth, other means to plug the void are alcohol, drug, noise, busyness, thrills of speed and violence, sexual orgy, self-inflicted pain, religious fantasies of heaven, and secular fantasies of utopia. How sad that so much effort, expense, and ingenuity are used to prevent the emergence of a self that, potentially, is only "a little lower than the angels." The hope that someday, with goodwill, we will no longer need these means of numbing and distraction is a fantasy, perhaps the wildest fantasy of all, for we appear to be born with certain defects, analogous to our body's susceptibility to hay fever and cancer, that, in the old days, were called sin.

Awareness, I have noted, offers us enormous advantages but also drawbacks. I have mentioned one drawback, that of forcing us to confront the emptiness at our core. Another is selectivity. It is not in itself a drawback, for unless much information is filtered out, our brain will be overwhelmed and made dysfunctional. That which we choose to be aware of is guided by its usefulness as we go about our business. Problematic is that the selectivity is also guided by psychological needs that are not immediately or obviously useful. They include the need to fill the void, the need to feel good about ourselves and our world, the need for self-esteem. When these are great, as they can be, the world we perceive turns unreal, even phantasmagorical. Much unhappiness, misunderstanding, and indeed evil occur because we dwell only on data that fatten our ego, not seeing even those closest to us as they are, much less the world as it is. Consider Eva Braun, Hitler's mistress. She was holed up in a bunker, together with others of Hitler's entourage, during the bombing of Berlin. Even with reality battering on her door, her awareness remained the small rosy world she had built around herself over a lifetime. To a friend she wrote pathetically: "I can't understand how all this can happen. It's enough to make me lose faith in God."

One type of selectivity—compartmentalization—deserves special mention because it so efficiently and totally excludes information unnecessary to the purpose at hand. Such efficient and total exclusion is also socially useful in that it prevents what we are in one area of life from spilling over to what we like to think we are in another. But that makes us all, to some degree, Dr. Jekyll and Mr. Hyde: one hour, I plunge my hand into the turkey to remove its innards, the next, I am a culinary artist adding an exotic herb to my creation; in the library, I am a fastidious scholar, in the bedroom, a sweaty naked animal; at home, I am a tender paterfamilias, at work, a hard boss. Hitler quite easily kept his horror of cruelty—his vegetarianism and abhorrence of hunting—separate from the mass murdering of Jews.

Gray Background

The human story is not, of course, all bleak. I now turn from the black backdrop to consider the gray. It is woven of acts of cooperation, of making and building, that are the obverses of hostility and destruction. Social animals, such as a species of ant in Australia, cooperate to build their worlds, including tall earth pillars that are their skyscrapers. We humans do likewise. Animals closest to us, the apes and chimpanzees, resemble us in other ways. They know maternal love and paternal protectiveness, they have a hierarchy of leaders and led. Beyond the biological family they form larger communities, knitted together by mutual help and an awareness of a hostile world beyond.

Naturally, there are important differences. One is that, although all social animals cooperate, humans do so to an exceptional degree. Cooperation on a large scale, quite apart from technological prowess, has given humans the power to radically transform the surface of the earth.[3] Something inherent in human nature, and not just culture, makes one person want to lend a hand in another's project when he happens to be standing by. Even a very young child, seeing a grown-up at work, toddles over to offer assistance, although the work being done has no obvious benefit to him. Nonhuman primates, under the same circumstance, mind their own business.[4] Of course, the larger human brain, endowed with the gift of language, greatly expands our species' ability to communicate and cooperate. But there must also be a willingness to engage others, including strangers and foreigners. More than other animals, humans show this willingness. They are willing not only because they can judge the usefulness of outsiders to them in case of need but also because they can see value in what outsiders make—their products. The latter gives humans an extra motivation to enlarge their social network that nonhuman animals lack. True, as I stressed earlier, people all too often and easily see outsiders as inferior or hostile, but they can also see them in a positive light as allies, trade partners, and friends. Nonkin of various categories may be added on in this way to a group made up originally of kinfolk, thus greatly increasing its size. Human groups can be larger—much larger—for another reason: technology. Whereas animals depend on the sounds they make and on face-to-face contact to keep in touch, humans have, in addition, numerous technocultural means.

Reciprocity, a basic principle of social behavior, is instinctive to animals. Among humans it is a custom so routinely practiced and so deeply ingrained that it, like following an instinct, is done without thinking. A good person is one who unquestioningly conforms to customs of mutual help and exchange as well as to other types of accepted behavior. A bad person, by contrast, is one who goes "up" or "over" the top, and this excess is, in fact, the root meaning of evil (Old Teutonic *ubiloz*). Large, stratified societies may have not only customs but written laws. A good citizen abides by both. A bad citizen is, again, one who goes "over the top," but there is this difference from the morality of small human groups. Going over the top in large sophisticated societies does not necessarily mean bad or evil. To the contrary, such a person may be commended for acting courageously in obedience to his or her conscience or to some higher principle and calling.

Going against customary good for a higher good is the sort of goodness I have been emphasizing, and I will have more to say about it later. Meanwhile, I need to stay in the gray background a little longer and make one more observation on reciprocity. This is its variety in the human species. Each human group has its own idea of reciprocation. Consider the etiquette of greeting. Between unequals, a difference in body language and gesture reinforces that status asymmetry. Sociobiologists find plentiful examples of such asymmetrical exchange in the animal world and like to point out that human nods and bows are just another example and therefore nothing special. Between equals, culture enables humans to come up with many different practices, all of which enforce the same relationship; in meeting an acquaintance or friend, for example, a person might shake hands or rub noses with the other person or clasp his or her own hands and bow. To sociobiologists this wide variety of greetings is, again, nothing special, for it reminds them of the variety they see in the animal world, forgetting—or choosing to overlook—the fact that among humans the variety is intraspecific.

Culture differentiates humans from other animals. This is particularly true in the moral sphere. Just as only humans possess language in the fullest sense of the word, so they—and only they—possess an innate sense of "good and bad," "right and wrong."[5] Not even the cleverest ape, Jerome Kagan reminds us, can be conditioned to be angry when it witnesses an injustice done to another. Sociobiologists, rather than note and draw implications from this important difference, choose instead to highlight similarities. They note that all primates, humans included, nurture and protect their young and that adult members cooperate—even to the degree of self-sacrifice—for the purpose of achieving common goals. These behaviors are admirable, and we may call them "moral," but it is a morality derived from biological drives and needs rather than from an intuition, one that can be elaborated into an ethic, of what is inherently right and what is inherently wrong. Is altruistic behavior susceptible to biological interpretation? To some, it is.[6] The question then arises, Is there anything at all in human conduct that goes beyond group survival and the successful transmission of a gene pool? Given our great propensity for evil, is it plausible that the virtues we share with other animals are sufficient in number and quality to help us reach our present high—but also highly defective—state? Or have we always benefited, in good times and bad (but especially in bad times), from unfathomable and unpredictable touches of grace?

Points of Light

I now turn to the points of light, and I will do so by shifting, for the nonce, my metaphor from spatial to temporal. The shift is not as large as it may seem at first, for my focus remains directed at phenomena that stand out—only now they stand out in a time line rather than in space.

Does human history have meaning? Does it show directional trend—progress? Even on the second, easier question, historians disagree. They may see progress in science and technology and broad directional shifts in such social measures as world population, life expectancy, and extent of urbanization, but few would say that the human story as a whole has meaning or shows progress.[7] Where do I stand? I have already revealed my pessimism in the night metaphor. As for humankind's movement through time, I cannot make overall sense of it. To me, it is not so much a story as the logorrhea of a madman, saved from collapse and meaninglessness by, paradoxically, disjunctures in the time line.

Certain disjunctures—also called high points—are widely recognized in world history. The first, if we start with ancient Egypt, is the appearance of the pharaoh Amenhotep IV, more widely known as Akhenaton. He lived in the fourteenth century BCE. He was a spiritual revolutionary who broke away from the polytheism of his fathers and nearly tore Egypt apart in his effort to establish the worship of a single god. "His monotheism," notes C. S. Lewis, "appears to have been of an extremely pure and conceptual kind. He did not . . . even identify God with the Sun. The visible disc was only His manifestation. It is an astonishing leap, more astonishing in some ways than Plato's, and, like Plato's, in sharp contrast to ordinary paganism."[8] Even a pharaoh couldn't change a whole people's way of thinking. After Akhenaton's death Egypt reverted to the much more familiar and comfortable idea of many gods.

Karl Jaspers famously identified a period in world history that he called the Axial Period, dating from 800 to 300 BCE.[9] Included in it are such luminaries as Homer, Isaiah, the Buddha, Confucius, Lao-tzu, Socrates, Plato, Aristotle, and Zeno. In different ways they lifted the human spirit to new heights: Homer gave us, in the *Iliad,* a portrait of transcendent justice; Isaiah, the suffering servant by whose strips we are healed; the Buddha, universal compassion; Confucius, civility as holy dance; Lao-tzu, weakness as strength; Socrates, philosophy as wisdom and ethics; Plato, the irresistible draw of the Good; Aristotle, natural philosophy; and Zeno, love of fate and homelessness as paths to virtue.

There was only one Axial Period, though other times have had their luminaries too. Jesus was certainly a luminary and is, moreover, Axial. He gave us the Sermon on the Mount; as for Axiality, calendars in most parts of the world are to this day divided by his brief time on earth. Since my purpose is to illustrate an idea rather than sketch a history, I'll skip the centuries to our own time. The twentieth century gave us Gandhi, Schweitzer, and Mandela. Each in his own way offered us a new understanding of goodness: Gandhi in his use of pacifism and peaceful protest to right wrong; Schweitzer in his reverence for all forms of life, which led to the modern environmental movement; Mandela in his demonstration that reconciliation and forgiveness not only are sublimely moral but also are powerful political tools.

Do all these people, who come from very different cultures and times, have anything in common? Surprisingly, they do. To start with what could seem just a curiosity, they were all physically vigorous. I have mentioned this quality in Confucius and Socrates, but the others, too, possessed it. There would seem to be a close relationship between physical and mental vitality, between vitality and self-confidence, between vitality and the ability to answer the revolutionary call. Mozart was joie de vivre incarnate: a social affair in his Vienna apartment started at six and ended at seven—seven in the morning! Keats, once considered a pale poet who lacked the will to live and died of consumption, struck his contemporaries as irrepressible. Schweitzer withstood punishing work. Weil, even under severe migraine, wrote reams of essays of unusual intellectual weight. Gandhi, to me, is a picture of wiry, indomitable strength: he had the strength to go on long protest marches. Mandela spent twenty-four years in prison yet could emerge from it to lead a peaceful revolution and then live on long past his tenure as president of the South African republic.

All six good people worked extremely hard and used their vitality to the full. One gets the impression that in every waking moment of his life Confucius sought to act in accordance with his precepts and, at every opportunity, add to his own knowledge of virtue and impart it to others. One feels convinced that Socrates never took time off from posing baffling questions to himself. Modern critics believe that Mozart, far from being merely God's scribe, taking down all but complete music effortlessly, slaved at his compositions, revising them many times, and that he in fact worked himself to death. Keats struggled to answer the urgent demands of his Muse while also finding time to look after his sick brother. Schweitzer was hard work incarnate—physical, mental, and spiritual. Simone Weil might be said to have died of exhaustion, having put more demands on her body than it could bear.

Yes, all six were undoubtedly hard workers, but they also showed a remarkable talent for enjoying the more sensual aspects of life. Relaxation doesn't seem the right word here, for it suggests a mere holding pattern before the next effort, whereas Confucius's lute playing, Socrates' lying about under a plane tree, Mozart's pranks and all-night parties, Keats's boxing and walking tours,

Schweitzer's attempt to make Bach sing on his jungle piano, and Weil's mild flirtations with young workers seem, in themselves, not time off but vital living.

Good people are childlike—or, rather, are like children before they become self-conscious. They are not afraid to be laughed at. They are so confident in who they are and what is right that they do not much care what others think. Confucius showed a "magnificent kind of ridiculousness" in his endless search, continuing into old age, for proper employment.[10] Socrates was occasionally a laughingstock to his more somber fellows. Mozart's high spirit was judged childlike or, worse, childish. Lincoln was, from time to time, a figure of fun, his ungainly height and looping gait contributing to it. But his action could also be a cause for amusement, such as when he left his friends to return a couple of stray birds to their mother. Schweitzer made it a part of his philosophy to do good, even if it should seem sentimental.

All six individuals I mentioned had an inclusive outlook on humanity and ethics; they were the least infected by the deadly virus of "us" and "them." Strongly individualistic themselves, they recognized others as individuals rather than as members of a class, race, or gender. Let me repeat, once more, the following extraordinary story. When the Vichy police came to Le Chambon and asked the villagers if they were hiding Jews, they could reply, truthfully from their point of view, "No," for they did not recognize the category "Jews." They recognized only a man, a woman, a child, each with a proper name, who happened to have knocked on their door.

Yet it is also true that good people acknowledge their roots, their indebtedness to what their ancestors have passed on to them. Confucius and Socrates, for all their boldness of thought, were pious. Socrates' allegiance to his beloved Athens was such that he refused to leave it even when he was placed under a death sentence. Even Jesus accepted his roots to the degree that he acknowledged the Davidic line and cried "Jerusalem, Jerusalem!" in anguish when he foresaw its destruction (Luke 14:34). Schweitzer lived in Africa for more than forty years but never lost his profound love for his native Alsace. Gandhi was a student in London and had lived in Africa, he was a Hindu who could also embrace Christianity, yet who could be more Indian? To the outside world he, with his loincloth and cotton spindle, was the very image of India. Mandela has become a world figure and world traveler, yet he retains a fondness and respect for his deceased father, who was a local chief, and for his homeland, Transkei.

Of the people I mentioned, Akhenaton and Zeno may be the exceptions. Akhenaton was a revolutionary of a stripe similar to Robespierre, Lenin, Stalin, and Mao. So far as we can judge, he had no respect for the past, no feeling of indebtedness to his predecessors. He seemed to have wanted a clean slate on which to build a new reality. Monotheism happens to appeal to most of us now, and for this reason we may be inclined to look favorably upon this Egyptian pharaoh. But he in his single vision could have been an ogre of destructiveness. As for Zeno, he lived in a time of turmoil when many people were on the move. Almost all his students came from elsewhere. His philosophy, which called for detachment, the ability to feel at home anywhere in the world, was noble but also rather joyless, perhaps because it sought too hard to rise above the basic human needs for piety and rootedness.

I exclude, reluctantly, Akhenaton from my list of good people and put Zeno in brackets. A good man is humble enough to acknowledge what the dead have given him and to recognize his strength (but also limitation) as the native of a particular place. Both traits are considered conservative. Yet a temperament touched by conservatism does not hinder a good man from thinking and acting with revolutionary boldness. What it does curb is megalomania—the passion to create a utopia on earth by force.[11]

Human goodness transcends time and place. It does so most clearly when it has its source in biology. True goodness—true moral excellence—is rare. We are therefore blessed in that at least biological goodness is something we can expect to encounter every day. No matter where we are in the world, babies in mothers' arms, children playing in a sandbox, and youngsters walking with natural ease and grace are there to console and invigorate us. We may be drawn to biology-based goodness for two other reasons besides beauty. One is that it is unconstrained by the social. The infant Anne smiling at me angelically while urinating is at the opposite pole of a social etiquette that exists largely to affirm status. Of course, Anne's behavior is charming only because it is confined to a fleeting phase of her life. Which leads to the second reason for admiring, with a touch of regret, biology-based goodness, and that is its transiency. In itself, transiency can make even repeated occurrences seem new, and for that, too, we should be grateful.

Another type of goodness that transcends time and place is the goodness of the obscure and humble. The metaphor "points of light" is clearly unsuitable here, for their goodness lies precisely in not shining, in not being highly visible, not even in the ways in which biology-based goodness is visible. We encounter such good men and women often enough in real life but, to our shame, overlook them. Literary works remind us of their existence. Melville's sailor Billy Budd, Dickens's maidservant and nurse Peggoty, Tolstoy's numerous peasant heroes, among them the soldier Platon and the boy serf Gerasim, are well-known examples. They all have a childlike quality; they all seem solid, without the "void" that taunts the more self-conscious; they are so unworldly that they could seem retarded, simpletons, God's fools, yet wise because they are free from the distorting lenses of power, wealth, and prestige. In the non-Western world, Taoism and Zen Buddhism see wisdom in a hermit singing in the rain, a monk eating a watermelon—people apparently without much learning or responsibility. Taoism is suspicious of the striving for knowledge that Confucianism recommends, and it is also suspicious of the social hierarchy that Confucianism takes for granted. It prefers people who stay at home, "content in their abode, and happy in the way they live, not bothering to travel to another country even when they could hear the dogs there barking." According to Zen Buddhism, goodness is paradoxically so deep that it is fit for the child at play. "Look children, Hailstones! Let's rush out," wrote the Japanese haiku poet Basho (1644–94).[12]

The goodness of the simple and the goodness of the child lie deep in both Western and Eastern thought. Simpleton and child are both ignorant, but their ignorance is not the ignorance of the stupid. André Trocmé, you remember, believed that human beings can be divided into more than the two categories "good" and "evil" and that there is a third—"stupidity." More often than not, stupidity carried out over the years rather than in a few egregious acts of evil enfeebles the fabric of society, making it liable to collapse with the slightest push from outside.[13] And so, what exactly is stupidity? How does it differ from ignorance and slowness of mind? A comparison with a quality in young children and Tolstoy's peasants is helpful. That quality is their openness to the world, their readiness to respond without prejudice. Their very ignorance—their not-knowing (their innocence)—makes this possible. In sharp contrast, the stupid are closed to the world, and if they respond to external events it is through a rigidly held position. The rigidity itself owes less to low IQ than to anxiety and fear and, under these burdens, a slavish need to conform. Here, then, is a sort of justice. A type of open attentiveness that, to Simone Weil, is prayer is not accessible to the stupid. It is, however, accessible to children, the uneducated, and even the mentally retarded, who, by means of it, gain a certain real, though not expressible, understanding of reality.

I now turn to behaviors that are exceptionally good, that stand out. They have one thing in common with biological and humble goodness, namely, they are not the product of a particular culture, time, or place. Take kindness to the stranger. In the Western world its locus classicus is the Good Samaritan. Unlike the priest and the Levite, who saw the wounded man by the road and walked to the other side, the Samaritan stopped to pour oil and wine on his wounds and bandaged them. He then put the man on his own animal and took him to an inn, where he cared for him (Luke 10:30–34). This happened—or could have happened—in ancient Palestine. Two millennia later, in a totally different place and culture, a Nepalese man, naked except for a threadbare loincloth, encountered a very sick American anthropologist. The Nepalese talked a local fisherman into lending him an outrigger canoe.

He put the American in the canoe and took him across sixty-five miles of monsoon-tossed sea to a hospital in Madras. The American said, "As he labored in the canoe, . . . it was completely clear to me that should the storm become violent, he would not hesitate to save me, at the risk of his own life."

Utterly selfless generosity occurs in societies that have little else in common. An Arab boy gave his last tattered shirt to a stranger. Scolded for his reckless giving, the boy looked bewildered and said, "But he asked, so how can I not give?" On the opposite side of the globe a white schoolteacher asked her black student to stop fidgeting in class. She had to make the request repeatedly. When she discovered that the source of the problem was the boy's malfunctioning kidney, which needed to be replaced, she simply offered one of her own. "Well, I have two. Do you want one?"

"Civility," a word that precedes "civilization," goes beyond the good manners I addressed earlier. It has a foundation in religion and philosophy, at the basis of which is the idea of equality, not just equality within a narrow rank or group but one, seldom precisely formulated, that is all-inclusive. Consider the importance of civility in ancient China and early modern France, two very different societies, and in our own time its advocacy in Czechoslovakia. Confucius made civility the centerpiece of his ethics. At its best, society was a holy dance in which everyone had a part and no part was without its dignity. Louis XIV would have approved of Confucian etiquette. The Sun King's court was run as an elaborate dance. In both premodern China and France, social inequality was tempered by the respect that the upper classes were urged to show those below them. In our time, notably uncivil academics of Marxist leaning dismiss good manners as merely a cover thrown over the ugly realities of power. This is not how Václav Havel sees it. He knows what it is like to live under communism and has come to think that, under it, one can suffer more from daily encounters with rudeness than from food shortages and other material deprivations. As president of Czechoslovakia, he urged his fellow citizens to practice good manners because they not only made social life more pleasant but could even promote economic enterprise and progress. For Havel himself, civility is a spiritual force, rooted in Christianity.[14]

Exceptionally good people, like intellectual and artistic geniuses, defy rational explanation; that is to say, we do not have a theory to account for their existence and cannot lay down precisely the conditions under which they will emerge. Good people themselves are famously unable to give the source of their action, just as creative geniuses are at a loss as to where their luminous ideas come from. The schoolboy Muggeridge walked into the sadistic headmaster's study, snatched the cane he was about to use on another boy, and broke it in two. Just like that. Jane Smith offered one of her kidneys to a sick student with the nonchalance of offering him a ride home. After World War II Magda Trocmé was asked so many times why she harbored Jewish refugees that she answered in exasperation, "I get pleasure from doing such things." Even the hardest decisions appear to come easily. British missionaries might pray all night for God's advice as to whether they should go to China, but Albert Schweitzer found it as natural as breathing to abandon a brilliant career for what he thought would be a lifetime of service in Africa. Most difficult of all is when the decision involves family members for whom one is responsible. A Dutch pastor in Nazi-occupied Holland was asked to help hide a Jewish baby. He struggled between compassion and fear. "No. Definitely not. We could lose our lives for that Jewish child!" Another man came in at this juncture. He took over the baby, looked into the little face, and said, "You say we could lose our lives for this child. I would consider that the greatest honor that could come to my family."

Acts of extraordinary goodness come from rich and poor, old and young, well educated and illiterate, religious and nonreligious. In common is that they are members of developed societies and of simpler societies that live at the margins of the developed ones. As for small, isolated groups—tribes in the premodern world, for example—acts of exceptional kindness are rare. The difference between them lies in the availability of opportunity.

In a small isolated group, a Nero is unlikely to emerge, and so heroic defiance will have no occasion to manifest itself. Nor can a woman offer her kidney to another when the technical means of transfer does not exist. Moreover, in a small group almost all members are bound by ties of kinship and honorary kinship, which means that help is, in a sense, always a help of self and its kin. Mutual care—the mother sacrificing herself for her offspring, the old limiting food for themselves so that the young can benefit, a hunter rescuing another hunter at the risk of his own life—is the sort of goodness that occurs in all functioning societies and indeed occurs in the animal kingdom. It is also the sort of goodness that scientists dwell on, perhaps because their biological model of evolutionary adaptation and change explains these acts in seeming total adequacy.

Developed societies (civilizations) offer sublime ideas of goodness that are, in their own way, as artificial as Mozart operas and Frank Gehry museums. One such idea is monotheism, which has the effect of demystifying the world, depleting it of gods and goddesses, and implying a certain equality among all people. If what we know of Akhenaton is true, monotheism appeared as a brief flash in ancient Egypt. It became a fixture in Judaism, Christianity, and Islam. Buddhism, Confucianism, and Taoism are not monotheistic, but they are universalist, and universalism has some of the same effects as monotheism. They all make little of the distinction between "us" and "them," they are individualistic to the extent that they all believe in the possibility of individual enlightenment, and they all urge that wealth, status, and prestige can be hindrances to such enlightenment. Lastly, in Buddhism and Taoism, if not in Confucianism, life itself does not greatly matter.

Developed societies may also offer philosophy, which, when it takes up moral questions, does so at a level far more abstract and universalist than are the customs and habits (mores) of a particular people. Because of its abstraction and universalism, the impact of moral philosophy on a people's outlook and behavior is weak— far weaker than that of religion, which, even if it is universalist, can make a direct emotional appeal through a combination of architecture, ritual, music, and stories. Religion's problem, insofar as it wants to retain its universalist orientation, is that it has come to depend too much on rituals and buildings. These, in part because of their aesthetic power to attract and hold, tend to narrow worshipers' field of attentiveness and make them grow attached to particular places rather than to otherworldly ideals. Stories by themselves run less risk of such attachments; they are less place-bound and can be as powerfully told under a tree, in the home, or in the market square as in a temple or in church.

Christianity is well known for its stories: it is the story of God coming down to earth to be incarnate as Man and as Suffering Servant save humans from their sins; it is the story of the Good

Samaritan, of the feeding of the five thousand, of raising Lazarus from the dead, of a Kingdom of God where the ideals in the Sermon on the Mount are a daily practice; it is even the utterly noncanonical story of the three kings visiting the babe in the manger, told even today in many parts of the world at Christmastime, reinforced by the jingle of sleigh bells, Mohr's "Silent Night," and Handel's *Messiah.* Stories—dramatic and epic—are, of course, central to Judaism. As for Hinduism and Buddhism, they too are given life by tales of Vishnu, the Buddha, and the bodhisattvas.

One can subconsciously learn from enthralling tales of this type. A man who, as a child, read Oscar Wilde's "The Happy Prince," a short story inspired by a mixture of Christianity and Buddhism, may forget entirely this source of his religiousness in adulthood; he becomes a good person, even a very good person, declaring that he has no religion or even that he is against religion. Similarly, people who live at the edge of a great civilization, say, American Indians, may have absorbed such values as universal human rights and the beauty of sacrificing oneself for a stranger while declaring that they abide solely by what their own ancestors have told them. By giving special credit to civilizations for producing exemplary goodness, I invite resentment from those who don't see themselves as members. All I can say is that high culture encourages extremes: bright lights shine against a background of intense darkness, acts of astonishing virtue alternate or stand side by side with acts of vomitous evil.

Allow me one last summary statement. A basic quality of good people is their fearlessness, which, ultimately, is an indifference to death. Good people, in their giving of self and openness to the world, often put their life at risk. In some ways, they are like children who do feats of daring from natural exuberance, and in other ways, like gifted athletes who in their striving for kinesthetic perfection jeopardize the possibility of a safe long life. Good people are exceptionally generous, and in this, too, they put their life at risk, for each real giving, whether of time, energy, or resource, is a mini-death. Generosity to one's kin and neighbors is understandable, for it is a requisite of communal life and well-being. Generosity to total strangers, especially when it occurs at the expense of one's own group, is harder to understand, and can seem "unnatural," almost a death-wish. Another way that good persons stand out is this. Even though they are unusually aware of their indebtedness to their group for the things they value—life, well-being, a past and a future—they nevertheless have the courage to stand apart from it and endure from its members ridicule, ostracism, and even exile—each in its own way a taste of death—in the name of conscience and an ineffable higher good. Good people, whether they know it or not, say it or not, act on the paradox that one gains life by losing it.

The universe is vast, pitch-black, cold, empty, and violent. On one speck of dust called Earth, life emerged to become successively plants, animals, and humans. Each step in the emergence takes the earth's living things closer to a more centered, conscious form of existence. Conscious life brings "light" into the universe. How little of it there is in the universe—and, for that matter, even on earth! Moreover, on earth, life's energies and their guiding light (consciousness) are used almost exclusively to serve the needs of survival and propagation. Only humans, with their higher consciousness, go beyond mere survival needs to engage in extreme acts of creativity and destruction, good and evil.

We who live on this planet may consider life here demanding and too often cheerless, yet being here at all remains the rarest of privilege, for where else in the universe would we rather be? Still, a sensitive individual is right to be appalled by not only the evil but also the drab wastefulness and mediocrity in so much of human life. Against this picture of reality—in part black, in part gray—are the pinpoints of light, jewels of human goodness. They may be natural phenomena, but they have the feel of epiphany, given us for balm, consolation, and, above all, hope.

Notes

Preface

1. Simone Weil, "Morality and Literature," in *On Science, Necessity, and the Love of God* (London: Oxford University Press, 1968), 160.

2. Stephen Jay Gould, "Ten Thousand Acts of Kindness," *Natural History* (December 1988): 12–17.

3. Eric Partridge, *Origins: A Short Etymological Dictionary of Modern English* (New York: Macmillan Company, 1958), 259.

Chapter 1. Vignettes: Range and Variety of Goodness

1. Jerome Kagan, "Human Morality," in *An Argument for Mind* (Cambridge, Mass.: Harvard University Press, 1998), 127–72; Richard A. Schweder, "Humans Really Are Different," *Science,* 5 February 1999, 798–99.

2. Maynard Solomon, *Mozart: A Life* (New York: HarperCollins, 1995), 4.

3. Norbert Elias, *Mozart: Portrait of a Genius* (Berkeley: University of California Press, 1993), 76.

4. Mary Gaitskill, "The Dream of Men," *New Yorker,* 23 November 1998.

5. George Steiner, *Errata* (New Haven, Conn.: Yale University Press, 1998), 43.

6. *New Yorker,* 4 July 1977, 19–20.

7. Malcolm Muggeridge, *Jesus: The Man Who Lives* (New York: Harper & Row, 1976), 113.

8. Apsley Cherry-Garrard, *The Worst Journey in the World* (New York: Carroll & Graff, 1989), 249, 256.

9. Paul Monette, *Becoming a Man* (New York: Harcourt Brace Jovanovich, 1992), 161–62.

10. *New Yorker,* 27 June 1977, 84.

11. Alex Shoumatoff, "The Ituri Forest," *New Yorker,* 6 February 1984, 88.

12. Alan Bennett, "What I Did in 1966," *London Review of Books,* 2 January 1997, 7.

13. W. H. Lewis, *The Splendid Century* (New York: Morrow Quill Paperback, 1978), 202.

14. Lance Morrow, in an interview with Václav Havel, *Time,* 3 August 1992, 48.

15. Václav Havel, *Summer Meditations* (New York: Vintage Books, 1993), 9, 15.

16. *The Diary of Virginia Woolf* (New York: Harcourt Brace Jovanovich, 1980), 3:73.

17. Antoine de Saint-Exupéry, *Wartime Writings, 1939–1944* (New York: Harcourt Brace Jovanovich, 1986), 110–11.

18. Tracy Kidder, "The Siege of Mirebalais," *New Yorker,* 17 April 1955, 77.

19. Alphonso Lingis, *The Community of Those Who Have Nothing in Common* (Bloomington: Indiana University Press, 1994), 158–59.

20. *New Yorker,* 9 July 1990, 25–26.

21. Richard Ellmann, *Oscar Wilde* (New York: Vintage Books, 1988), 269.

22. Arnold Toynbee, *Acquaintances* (New York: Oxford University Press, 1967), 89–90.

23. *Science,* 13 May 1988, 876.

24. Iris Murdoch, *Metaphysics as a Guide to Morals* (New York: Allen Lane/Penguin Press, 1992), 430.

25. F. A. Worsley, *Endurance: An Epic of Polar Adventure* (New York: Norton, reprinted 1999), 97.

26. Albert Schweitzer, *A Place for Revelation: Sermons on Reverence for Life* (New York: Macmillan, 1988), 120.

27. Albert Schweitzer, *Memoirs of Childhood and Youth* (Syracuse, N.Y.: Syracuse University Press, 1977), 79.

28. Robert Coles, *Dorothy Day: A Radical Devotion* (Reading, Mass.: Addison-Wesley, 1987), 43.

29. *Tolstoy's Diaries,* ed. and trans. R. F. Christian (London: Flamingo, 1994), 397.

30. Albert Schweitzer, *Civilization and Ethics* (New York: Macmillan, 1929), 267.

31. William James, *Essays on Faith and Morals* (New York: New American Library, 1974), 19–20.

32. John Cowper Powys, *Autobiography* (Colgate: Colgate University Press, 1994), 276–77.

33. Tzvetan Todorov, *Facing the Extreme* (New York: Metropolitan Books, 1996), 202.

34. Mother Teresa, *No Greater Love* (Novato, Calif.: New World Library, 1997), 55.

35. See Jill Haak Adels, *The Wisdom of the Saints* (Oxford: Oxford University Press, 1987), 45.

36. See Josef Pieper, *Death and Immortality* (South Bend, Ind.: St. Augustine Press, 2000), 5.

37. Helen Dukas and Banish Hoffman, eds., *Albert Einstein: The Human Side* (Princeton, N.J.: Princeton University Press, 1989), 23, 102.

38. *Psychology Today* (September 1983): 30, 32.

39. *New Yorker,* 27 September 1997, 53.

40. *New York Times,* 4 August 1991.

41. Garry Wills, *Lincoln at Gettysburg* (New York: Simon & Schuster, 1992), 34; Brand Blanshard, *Four Reasonable Men* (Amherst: Wesleyan University Press, 1984), 257.

42. William Stringfellow, *My People Is the Enemy* (New York: Doubleday Anchor, 1966), 45.

43. Wilfred Thesinger, *Arabian Sands* (New York: Dutton, 1959), 123–24.

44. James, *Essays on Faith and Morals,* 195.

45. Hannah Arendt, *Responsibility and Judgment* (New York: Schocken Books, 2003), 63.

46. *New Yorker,* 19 August 1985, 20.

47. Simone Pétrement, *Simone Weil: A Life* (New York: Pantheon Books, 1976), 416.

48. Bruce Schechter, *My Brain Is Open* (New York: Simon & Schuster, 1998), 17, 161–62.

49. *New York Times,* 18 December 1999.

50. *Charles Darwin's Autobiography* (New York: Collier Books, 1961), 70.

51. John Jay Chapman, "William James," in *The Oxford Book of Essays,* ed. John Gross (Oxford: Oxford University Press, 1992), 338.

52. John Bayley, *Elegy for Iris* (New York: St. Martin's Press, 1999), 66, 169.

53. A. N. Wilson, *C. S. Lewis* (New York: Norton, 1990), 145.

54. Ray Monk, *Ludwig Wittgenstein: The Duty of Genius* (New York: The Free Press, 1990), 83.

55. Wendy Doniger's response to J. M. Coetzee, *The Lives of Animals* (Princeton, N.J.: Princeton University Press, 1999), 93.

56. J. B. Pratt, *The Pilgrimage of Buddhism* (New York: Macmillan, 1928), 93.

57. Edward A. Armstrong, *Saint Francis: Nature Mystic* (Berkeley: University of California Press, 1976), 143–44, 170–71.

58. Joshua Wolf Shenk, *Lincoln's Melancholy* (Boston: Houghton Mifflin, 2005), 15, 29.

59. Schweitzer, *Memoirs,* 37.

60. Norman Cousins, *Albert Schweitzer's Mission: Healing and Peace* (New York: Norton & Company, 1985), 56.

61. Gustave Flaubert, *Three Tales* (New York: New Directions, 1924), 119–21.

62. Dorothy Day, *Loaves and Fishes* (San Francisco: Harper & Row, 1983), 78–79.

63. *Minneapolis Tribune,* 23 September 1970.

64. Gregory Wolfe, *Malcolm Muggeridge: A Biography* (Grand Rapids, Mich.: Eerdmans, 1997), 23.

65. Simone Weil, *Seventy Letters* (London: Oxford University Press, 1965), 107.

66. George Orwell, *Homage to Catalonia* (London: Secker & Warburg, 1938), 1.

67. Robert H. Frank, *Passions within Reason* (New York: Norton, 1988), 212.

68. *New Republic,* 3 February 1982.

69. Wolfe, *Malcolm Muggeridge,* 353.

70. Jean Lacouture, *De Gaulle: The Ruler of 1945–1970* (New York: Norton, 1991), 294–300.

71. *New York Times,* 23 July 2006.

Chapter 2. Doing Good in the Midst of Evil

1. Corrie ten Boom, *The Hiding Place* (New York: Bantam Books, 1971), 99.

2. David P. Gushee, *The Righteous Gentiles of the Holocaust: A Christian Interpretation* (Minneapolis: Fortress Press, 1994), 159.

3. Philip Hallie, *Lest Innocent Blood Be Shed* (New York: Harper/Perennial, 1994), 65.

4. Ibid., 154.

5. Tzvetan Todorov, *Facing the Extreme* (New York: Metropolitan Books, 1996), 227.

6. Hallie, *Lest Innocent Blood Be Shed,* 155.

Chapter 3. Good Individuals: Their Life Stories

1. *The Li Chi,* trans. James Legge, in *Sacred Books of the East* (London, 1885; reprinted, 1926), 3:369.

2. *The Analects of Confucius,* trans. Chichung Huang (New York: Oxford University Press, 1997), 7:26. Hereafter cited in text.

3. Jonathan Clements, *Confucius: A Biography* (Phoenix Mill: Sutton Publishing, 2004), 68.

4. Herbert Fingarette, *Confucius—The Secular as Sacred* (New York: Harper Torchbooks, 1972).

5. H. G. Creel, *Confucius: The Man and the Myth* (London: Routledge & Kegan Paul, 1951), 22.

6. Ibid., 61.

7. Clements, *Confucius,* 31.

8. Creel, *Confucius,* 64.

9. Plato *Phaedrus* 230d.

10. Xenophon *Oeconomicus* 5, 6.9.

11. Micheline Sauvage, *Socrates and the Human Conscience* (New York: Harper & Brothers, 1960), 50.

12. W. K. C. Guthrie, *Socrates* (Cambridge: Cambridge University Press, 1971).

13. Plato *Symposium* 215b.

14. Plato *Republic* 403a–c; Plato *Laws* 838e.

15. Karl Jaspers, *Socrates, Buddha, Confucius, Jesus* (San Diego: Harvest Book, 1990), 8.

16. Xenophon *Memorabilia.*

17. Gregory Vlastos, *Socrates: Ironist and Moral Philosopher* (Ithaca, N.Y.: Cornell University Press, 1991).

18. Jean Brun, *Socrates* (New York: Walker and Company, 1962), 13–14.

19. Plato *Phaedo* 118; A. E. Taylor, *Socrates: The Man and His Thought* (Garden City, N.Y.: Doubleday Anchor, 1952); on the question "What Kind of a Man Is He?" see Gregory Vlastos's introduction in his *Philosophy of Socrates: A Collection of Critical Essays* (New York: Anchor, 1971).

20. Norbert Elias, *Mozart: Portrait of a Genius* (Berkeley: University of California Press, 1993), 80–81.

21. Maynard Solomon, *Mozart: A Life* (New York: HarperCollins, 1995), 89.

22. Ibid., 319.

23. Ibid., 401.

24. Peter Gay, *Mozart* (New York: Lipper/Viking, 1999), 25.

25. Hans Mersmann, ed., *Letters of Wolfgang Amadeus Mozart* (New York: Dover, 1972), 262.

26. Solomon, *Mozart,* 312.

27. Ibid., 318.

28. Mersmann, *Letters,* 184.

29. Solomon, *Mozart,* 459.

30. Ibid., 481.

31. Gay, *Mozart,* 3, 131.

32. Marion Vera Forster, in the pamphlet that accompanies the DVD *A Mozart Celebration from Stephansdom* (EuroArts, 2006).

33. *Complete Poems and Selected Letters of John Keats,* introduction by Edward Hirsch (New York: Modern Library, 2001), 236, 249, 224.

34. *The Selected Letters of John Keats,* edited and introduced by Lionel Trilling (New York: Farrar, Straus and Young, 1951), 15.

35. Ibid., 154.

36. Ibid., 168.

37. Ibid., 80, 140–41.

38. "To My Brothers," in *Complete Poems,* 41–42.

39. *Selected Letters,* 73, 189.

40. Ibid., 244.

41. "La Belle Dame Sans Merci," in *Complete Poems,* 354.

42. Andrew Motion, *Keats: A Biography* (New York: Farrar, Straus and Giroux, 1998); Robert M. Ryan, *Keats: The Religious Sense* (Princeton, N.J.: Princeton University Press, 1976); Robert M. Ryan and Ronald A. Sharp, eds., *The Persistence of Poetry: Bicentennial Essays on Keats* (Amherst: University of Massachusetts Press, 1998).

43. Asen Balikci, *The Netsilik Eskimo* (New York: Natural History Press, 1970), 218–20.

44. E. E. Evans-Pritchard, *The Nuer* (Oxford: Clarendon Press, 1940), 27.

45. Edward A. Armstrong, *Saint Francis: Nature Mystic* (Berkeley: University of California Press, 1976), 110–11.

46. Albert Schweitzer, *A Place for Revelation: Sermons on Reverence for Life* (New York: Macmillan, 1988), 24.

47. Albert Schweitzer, *Memoirs of Childhood and Youth* (Syracuse, N.Y.: Syracuse University Press, 1977), 15–17.

48. Ibid., 37–38.

49. Albert Schweitzer, *Out of My Life and Thought* (Baltimore, Md.: Johns Hopkins University Press, 1998), 155.

50. Schweitzer, *A Place for Revelation,* 15–16.

51. Ibid., 31.

52. James Bentley, *Albert Schweitzer: The Enigma* (New York: Harper-Collins, 1992), 145.

53. Schweitzer, *Out of My Life,* 81.

54. James Brabazon, *Albert Schweitzer: A Biography* (Syracuse, N.Y.: Syracuse University Press, 2000), 439–40.

55. Bentley, *Albert Schweitzer,* 10.

56. Schweitzer, *Out of My Life,* 141.

57. Ibid., 147.

58. Brabazon, *Albert Schweitzer,* 406, 408, 452.

59. Schweitzer, *Out of My Life,* 176.

60. Schweitzer, *A Place for Revelation,* 76–77.

61. Reprinted in Schweitzer, *Out of My Life,* 58–59.

62. Charles R. Joy, *Music in the Life of Albert Schweitzer* (Boston: Beacon Press, 1959), 6.

63. Ibid., 119–21.

64. T. S. Eliot, "Preface," in Simone Weil, *The Need for Roots* (Boston: Beacon Press, 1955), vi.

65. Simone Pétrement, *Simone Weil: A Life* (New York: Pantheon Books, 1976), 8, 20.

66. Jacques Cabaud, *Simone Weil* (London: Harvill Press, 1964), 18.

67. *The Notebooks of Simone Weil* (London: Routledge & Kegan Paul, 1956), 2:537.

68. Richard Rees, *Simone Weil: A Sketch for a Portrait* (Carbondale: Southern Illinois University Press, 1966), 20.

69. Simone Weil, *Waiting for God* (New York: Capricorn Books, 1959), 64.

70. Weil, *Need for Roots,* 233–34.

71. Ibid., 235.

72. Marjorie Hope Nicolson, "The Circle of Perfection," in *The Breaking of the Circle* (New York: Columbia University Press, 1960), 47–80.

73. Weil, *Waiting for God,* 131–32.

74. Pétrement, *Simone Weil,* 124.

75. Weil, *On Science, Necessity & the Love of God* (London: Oxford University Press, 1968), 14–15.

76. Weil, *Waiting for God,* 129.

77. Cabaud, *Simone Weil,* 5.

78. Pétrement, *Simone Weil,* 302–3.

79. Ibid., 306, 309–10.

80. Weil, *Waiting for God,* 67–68.

81. George Herbert, *The Temple* (London: Nonesuch Press, 1927, printed from MS, 1633), 185.

82. Cabaud, *Simone Weil,* 168–70.

83. Pétrement, *Simone Weil,* 333.

Chapter 4. Reflections

1. Yi-Fu Tuan, *Dominance and Affection: The Making of Pets* (New Haven, Conn.: Yale University Press, 1984).

2. A neat example of flattering self-image comes from the northwestern quarter of New Mexico. The five groups of people who live there have, in each case, a word for themselves that implies their superiority. The Navaho call themselves *dineh* (the people); the Zuni call themselves *ashiwi* (the cooked ones); the Mormons refer to themselves as "the chosen people"; the Hispanics are *la gente,* "people" in the honorific sense; the Texans consider themselves "real" or "super" Americans, the only really white Americans. See Evon Z. Vogt and Ethel M. Albert, *People of Rimrock* (Cambridge, Mass.: Harvard University Press, 1966), 26.

3. Lewis Mumford, *The Myth of the Machine* (New York: Harcourt, Brace & World, 1966).

4. John B. Silk, "Who Are More Helpful, Humans or Chimpanzees?" *Science,* 3 March 2006, 1248–49.

5. Jerome Kagan, "Human Morality," in *An Argument for Mind* (Cambridge, Mass.: Harvard University Press, 1998), 127–72.

6. S. A. Boorman and P. R. Levitt, *The Genetics of Altruism* (New York: Academic Press, 1980); Frans de Waal, *Our Inner Ape* (New York: Riverhead Books, 2005); Lee Alan Dugatkin, *The Altruism Equation* (Princeton, N.J.: Princeton University Press, 2006).

7. Julian L. Simon, ed., *The State of Humanity* (Cambridge: Blackwell, 1995); Robert D. Sack, ed., *Progress: Geographical Essays* (Baltimore, Md.: Johns Hopkins University Press, 2002).

8. C. S. Lewis, *Reflections on the Psalms* (London: Fontana Books, 1961), 74.

9. Karl Jaspers, *The Origin and Goal of History* (New Haven, Conn.: Yale University Press, 1953), 1–21.

10. Creel, *Confucius: The Man and the Myth* (London: Routledge & Kegan Paul, 1951), 61.

11. Jay Winter, *Dreams of Peace and Freedom: Utopian Moments in the Twentieth Century* (New Haven, Conn.: Yale University Press, 2006).

12. *Tao Te Ching* (Harmondsworth, Middlesex: Penguin Classics, 1963), chap. 80; Christmas Humphreys, *Zen Buddhism* (New York: Macmillan, 1962), 81.

13. See Mary McCarthy's reflections on stupidity and wickedness in Carol Brightman, ed., *Between Friends: The Correspondence of Hannah Arendt and Mary McCarthy, 1949–1975* (New York: Harcourt, Brace & Company, 1995), 296–97.

14. Edward Shils, "Civility and Civil Society: Good Manners between Persons and Concern for the Common Good in Public Life," in Steven Grosby, ed., *The Virtue of Civility* (Indianapolis: Liberty Fund, 1997), 63–102.

Index

Abbey, Richard, 125

aesthetic-moral appreciation: as goodness, 4–8; music as salvatory, 116

aesthetics: beauty as inspiration to goodness, 99–100; erōs as response to beauty or moral goodness, 99–100; politics and good taste, 19–20. *See also* aesthetic-moral appreciation

AIDS, 41–42

Akhenaton (Amenhotep IV), 195–96, 200–201, 208

altruism, 194

animals: animal rights movement, 133–34; Christian thought and treatment of, 137–38, 144; Confucius and role of natural world, 84, 87; experimentation on, 143; as food source, 135–36, 143, 186; humans as distinct from other, 4, 186–87, 193–94; indebtedness to, 136, 143–44; as lacking sense of justice, 4, 142, 194; Lincoln as respectful of and kind to, 55–56; morality expressed through respect for, 134–36; motives for kindness toward,

54–55; respect for, 53–57, 134–36, 139; Schweitzer and ethical treatment of, 56, 64, 134–36, 138–40, 143–44; "sentiment of honor" and gratitude toward, 34–35; slaughter of, 143, 185–86; Weil's opinion on, 161–62

annihilation of the will, 41

Antarctica, exploration of, 9–11, 30–31

Arabian Sands (Thesinger), 45–46

Ardoin, John, 53

art: performance as generosity, 52–53. *See also* music

athleticism, 7–8, 105

Augustine, Saint, 38

Auschwitz, 35–36

awareness, 186–89

Axial Period of human development, 196–97

babies or infants, 5, 105, 201–2

Bailey, Benjamin, 127

Bamford, James, 67

Barenboim, Daniel, 117